W9-CLD-767

LONELY PLANET
ROAD TRIP
BLUES & BBQ

Tom Downs

92 Park Street · Adams, MA 01220
phone · 413 743-8345

Road Trip Blues & BBQ
1st edition – January 2005

Published by Lonely Planet Publications Pty Ltd
ABN 36 005 607 983

Australia	Head Office, Locked Bag 1, Footscray, Vic 3011
	☎ 03 8379 8000 fax 03 8379 8111
	🖥 talk2us@lonelyplanet.com.au
USA	150 Linden St, Oakland, CA 94607
	☎ 510 893 8555 toll free 800 275 8555
	fax 510 893 8572
	🖥 info@lonelyplanet.com
UK	72–82 Rosebery Avenue, London EC1R 4RW
	☎ 020 7841 9000 fax 020 7841 9001
	🖥 go@lonelyplanet.co.uk

This title was commissioned in Lonely Planet's Oakland office and produced by: **Commissioning Editor** & **Project Manager** Kathleen Munnelly **Series & Cover Designer** Candice Jacobus **Regional Publishing Manager** David Zingarelli.

Freelancers: Cartographer Bart Wright **Layout Designer** Hayley Tsang **Editor** Valerie Sinzdak **Indexer** Ken DellaPenta **Proofer** Michele Posner

Cover photograph Neon Light on Beale Street – Memphis, Tennessee, Greg Elms/Lonely Planet Images. All images are copyright of the photographers unless otherwise indicated. This image is available for licensing from Lonely Planet Images:
🖥 www.lonelyplanetimages.com

ISBN 1 74059 574 2

Printed through The Bookmaker International Ltd. Printed in China

CONTENTS

FROM THE PUBLISHER

AUTHOR

Tom Downs

Tom Downs was introduced to Mississippi unexpectedly when his car broke down on I-55, somewhere in Yalobusha County, en route from Memphis to New Orleans. 'It was high noon in July,' he recalls, 'and I had some walking to do to get to a service station that appeared to double as an automotive graveyard. Old sedans and trooper cars overgrown with vines. It was a hallucinogenic experience for a Californian like me.' Tom's car avoided the same fate, but needless to say, he fell in love with the place. He also has an abiding affection for blues music and, to hear him tell it, 'pork prepared every which way.' Tom is author of several Lonely Planet guidebooks, including *New Orleans* and *Ireland*. He lives in Berkeley, CA, with his wife and children.

Heartfelt gratitude to Charlie Patton, Robert Johnson, Skip James and countless others, and to those who recorded them. Mississippi has inspired some great books (fiction and non-fiction, as well as some great guides). I think I read them all, so thanks to the writers who inspired me. Love to Fawn, Mai, Lana and Liam.

SEND US YOUR FEEDBACK

We love to hear from travelers – your comments keep us on our toes and help make our books better. Our well-traveled team reads every word on what you loved or loathed about this book. Although we cannot reply individually to postal submissions, we always guarantee that your feedback goes straight to the appropriate authors, in time for the next edition – and the most useful submissions are rewarded with a free book. To send us your updates – and find out about LP events, newsletters and travel news – visit our award-winning website: 🖥 **www.lonelyplanet.com.**

Note: We may edit, reproduce and incorporate your comments in Lonely Planet products such as guidebooks, websites and digital products, so let us know if you don't want your comments reproduced or your name acknowledged. For a copy of our privacy policy visit 🖥 www.lonelyplanet.com/privacy.

HOW TO USE THIS BOOK

Opening hours for places listed in this book apply during summer, except where otherwise noted. When entry fees are not listed, sites are free (although some may request a small donation). Price gradings (eg $10/7/5) indicate admission for adults/students & seniors/children.

Text Symbols

☎	telephone	s	single rooms
🖥	internet available	d	double rooms
⏲	opening hours	ste	suites
Ⓟ	parking available	dm	dorm beds
🏊	swimming pool		

INTRODUCTION

The blues are often called the taproot of American popular music, but they were once a regional folk idiom played by some of the world's poorest people. In the land where the blues began, time stands as still as cypress stumps in stagnant water. Dirt-poor, rural, left for the kudzu – that pretty well describes much of the Mississippi Delta. It's an oddly appealing motley of cotton fields, agricultural refuse and early-20th-century towns inclined to lean backwards no matter which way the buildings are tilting. Ongoing economic decline is evident in the rows of abandoned shops and run-down houses and groups of people standing around on street corners. Long-abandoned commissaries and rusted farm equipment pop up along the road, and painted signs fade away on the sides of buildings. In such a place, one can easily imagine that the blues rises from the ground and hangs over everything.

The Delta, stretching for 250 miles from Memphis, Tennessee, to Vicksburg, Mississippi, is an alluvial plain rather than an actual river delta, and the soil deposited over millennia by the Mississippi River is among the richest in the world. To Southern landowners in the late 19th century, that meant it was ideal for planting cotton. The labor force that worked the cotton, of course, were African-Americans – former slaves, the children of slaves, the grandchildren of slaves. They were sharecroppers now, but most of them remained desperately poor.

Yet some managed to scrape up enough money for a Stella guitar or a Hohner harmonica. They sang in a style reminiscent of old field hollers, prison songs and levee camp songs. This new music contained echoes of Africa, but spoke directly of their experience in the New World. Their blues were by turns tragic, disquieting, weary, spiritual, belligerent and uplifting.

Most visitors come looking for remnants of this past, and with a willingness to venture from Hwy 61, the so-called Blues Highway, they find it. They'll also find lots of life in the Delta. Mississippi may be an intense place, but Mississippians are friendly people who more often than not welcome a stranger with cold beer, tender barbecue and blues grooves in shambling juke joints.

For the motorist, the Delta naturally links Memphis and New Orleans. Hwys 61, 49 and 1 form an axis through this most musically inclined of regions. It's all packed within a few hundred miles – a couple of days' driving if you only have a short time, or two full weeks of journeying, juking and eating your way through a fascinating slice of America.

GETTING THERE & AROUND

The two major airports in this region are **Memphis International Airport** (☎ 901-922-8000; 2491 Winchester Rd) and **Louis Armstrong New Orleans International Airport** (☎ 504-464-0831; www.flymsy.com; 900 Airline Hwy). These airports mostly handle domestic flights, so

Blues Timeline

1860–64 Civil War results in abolishment of slavery.

1890s Blues and jazz develop simultaneously in the southern US.

1896 US Supreme Court decision Plessy v Ferguson institutionalizes segregation.

1903 WC Handy hears blues for first time and eventually helps popularize the music.

1918 Charlie Patton established as hottest blues man in the mid-Delta.

1920s Bessie Smith, the 'Empress of the Blues,' is the highest-paid black entertainer in the US.

1927–30 Sales of 'race' records reach peak levels; Delta blues are finally widely recorded.

1936–38 Robert Johnson records fewer than 40 songs, then dies mysteriously.

1942 Muddy Waters records country blues for the Library of Congress.

1944 Mechanical cotton-picker introduced on Hopson Plantation; spells the end of the sharecropper system. Northern migration of blacks hits full stride.

1950s In Chicago, Mississippi-born musicians establish a modern, electric blues sound that will become popular worldwide.

1960s Folk revival leads to 'rediscovery' of many early Delta blues masters, such as Son House, Skip James and Mississippi John Hurt.

1968 In Memphis, Dr Martin Luther King Jr is assassinated on April 4.

travelers from Europe or Asia will likely change planes on the East or West Coast. **Jackson Airport** (☎ 601-939-5631), just southeast of the Mississippi Delta, is also served by most major US airlines.

The only way to really explore the Delta is by car. Dozens of rental car companies are stationed at the airports, and most require a credit card and proof that you're over 25 years old. The major rental agencies include **Alamo** (☎ 800-327-9633; www.alamo.com), **Avis** (☎ 800-321-3721; www.avis.com), **Budget** (☎ 800-527-0700; www.budget.com), **Dollar** (☎ 800-800-4000; www.dollar.com), **Hertz** (☎ 800-654-3131; www.hertz.com), **National** (☎ 800-328-4567; www.nationalcar.com) and **Thrifty** (☎ 800-367-2277; www.thrifty.com). The cheapest companies (Alamo, Dollar) charge $120 to $200 per week, plus about $200 for one-way rentals. The stretch of I-55 from Memphis to New Orleans is easily driven in a day, so returning your car is doable and cost-effective (your flight will likely cost less as well).

If you're going to drive your own car, it makes sense to join the **American Automobile Association** (AAA; ☎ 800-922-8228; www.aaa.com; annual membership $50). AAA provides minor breakdown assistance, short-distance towing and free highway maps.

If Chicago is also in your plans, consider taking **Amtrak** (☎ 901-526-0052; 545 S Main St) to or from Memphis, thus roughly following the route so many African Americans took in their migration to the great Midwest city.

ITINERARIES

This book is organized as a north-south trip from Memphis to New Orleans. Of course, you can do it in the other direction, but if you begin from Memphis, you'll reach the heart of the Mississippi Delta much more quickly.

STRAIGHT SHOT OF BLUES

With only two days, one can dip a toe into the Delta by spending a night in **Memphis** and a night in **Clarksdale**. These rockin' towns are just an hour's drive apart, and both are goldmines of jukes, barbecue joints, nightclubs, tuneful museums and music history.

HWY 61 REVISITED

Four or five days is enough to drive Hwys 61 and 49E from **Memphis** to **New Orleans**, spending a night in each of those great cities and stopping over in two or three Delta towns. Make 'em **Clarksdale**, **Greenwood** and (in a five-day plan) **Natchez**. At any point in Mississippi, you can cut over to I-55 and get to New Orleans in just a few hours.

SCOURING THE LAND OF THE BLUES

The Memphis–New Orleans axis can keep you busy for ten days or two weeks if you're really into it. **Memphis** is properly done in two nights, and the Shack Up Inn in **Clarksdale** makes an ideal two-night base for checking out the town and the upper Delta.

Tool along **Highways 1** and **49W** – rustic rural backroads that conjure images of the 1930s – and stop in all the dilapidated towns that time seems to have forgotten: **Helena, Merigold, Rosedale, Indianola, Greenwood, Bentonia** and countless others. Spend a night at the Sun-n-Sand Motel in **Jackson** and have a few hi-balls in the surreal lounge.

Bop through the Old South of **Vicksburg** and **Natchez**, do a night in **Opelousas**, Louisiana, for zydeco, and spend as long as you like in **New Orleans**. You'll never get bored. With a few advance calls, you can find out when live music is happening and plan an amazing trip around that.

HIGHLIGHTS

Old Hwy 61 (p18): The eerie old road still exists in parts of the northern Delta. Hwy 1 (p24) along the Mississippi River has a similar, two-lane appeal.

Memphis barbecue (p13): You can't beat the meat in this town – pork shoulder sandwiches and baby-back ribs to make you forget your blues.

Clarksdale's Shack Up Inn (p28): Sleeping in a restored (and updated) sharecropper's cabin adds historic perspective to the blues pilgrimage.

Greenwood's classic restaurants (p43): With atmospheric old spots like Lusco's and the Crystal Grill, you'd think Greenwood has enough, but don't overlook the town's great little barbecue and soul food joints.

Haunted graveyards: Pay your respects at the graves of long-gone blues greats like Memphis Minnie (p18), Charlie Patton (p39), Mississippi John Hurt (p45) and Robert Johnson (p42).

Thursdays at Poor Monkey Lounge (p34): Looking for a tumble-down juke along an unpaved road amid cotton fields? Look no further.

Margaret's Grocery (p49): This surreal religious monument was fashioned out of an old grocery store and a broken-down bus outside Vicksburg.

New Orleans nightlife (p60): The Crescent City lays it on thick with jazz, blues, R&B, salsa, zydeco and soul music pretty much every night.

Blues Primer

Traditional blues forms borrowed freely from other musical styles, including work songs, rags and minstrel ditties. Early blues musicians like Charlie Patton frequently mixed songs from all of these styles into an evening's set. There's no single style of blues, but a few signature elements make a basic blues song easily identifiable.

Blues guitar and harmonica typically are played as voices responding to the lyrics. A vocal line is followed by a musical line, and the two interrelate almost like singers in call-and-response music.

The most easily recognized blues song follows a 12-bar structure, which can be repeated over and over. Within that framework, the most common blues verse structure is A-A-B, in which the first two lines are identical (or nearly so) and the concluding line rhymes with the first two:

Woke up this morning with the blues all 'round my bed
Woke up this morning with the blues all 'round my bed
I ache so bad, Lord, got a sandbag on my head

Rhythmically, the oldest Delta blues are sometimes slow and repetitive, not unlike the steady turning of an oxcart's wheels or the swinging of an axe into a tree. As the 20th century gathered momentum, these slow rhythms gave way to more energetic locomotive tempos that reflected the reality of black migration within the Delta and beyond, to places like Chicago.

That said, many songs are recognized as blues without adhering to any of these conventions. When you get right down to it, the heart of the blues is its emotional depth. Blues singers and musicians live by the 'blue notes,' which are notes packed with feeling that fall in between the notes on the western scale. On a guitar, a blue note is played by bending a string until the note rises to a satisfying place somewhere between two frets. A very bluesy song can consist of blue notes – and, more importantly, blues feeling – without following traditional blues forms.

MEMPHIS, TN

Population 650,100; Map 2

Memphis has been steeped in blues and nourished on barbecue. It has served potent rock and roll hi-balls and dug its gospely grooves into the soul of America. The assassination of Dr Martin Luther King Jr here in 1968 left a wound that the nation is still trying to heal.

Memphis' location on the Mississippi River, immediately north of the Mississippi Delta, made it a natural conduit for the transport of cotton and blues. The same northward pull that drew so many Mississippi blacks to Chicago during the first half of the 20th century attracted many to Memphis, which maintained a two-way cultural link with Delta towns just a few hours' drive away.

The black community thrived in the city, and Beale St was its principal hub of business and entertainment. Gin joints and bordellos offered ample employment to musicians, and the district's cabarets and theaters featured star performers like Bessie Smith, Ma Rainey and Memphis Minnie.

Memphis was at the epicenter of early rock and roll as well. Sam Phillips opened Sun Studios to record black musicians, and some of their electrified blues sound a lot like the beginnings of rock. When Elvis Presley strolled into Phillips' studio in 1954, rock catapulted right into the American mainstream. Today, Presley's spangly cape seems to arch over the city like a casino in the sky. But the King's legacy is deeply imbued with African American rhythms and gospel feeling, which he absorbed in Memphis.

SIGHTS

Memphis is stacked with enough commemorative museums and historic sites to keep a music-mad traveler happy for days. Also be sure to check out the Lorraine Motel, where Dr Martin Luther King Jr was shot, for a chilling trip back to that fateful day in 1968.

GRACELAND

☎ 901-332-3322, 800-238-2000; www.elvis.com; 3734 Elvis Presley Blvd; admission mansion $18, memorabilia collection $6, car museum $8, aircraft collection $7, all attractions $27; ♥ 9am-5pm Mon-Sat & 10am-4pm Sun Mar-Oct, 10am-4pm Mon, Wed-Sun Nov-Mar

For an utterly fascinating insight into a great American success story, do not miss the chance to see Graceland.

Elvis bought the house and 500-acre farm surrounding it in 1957, after recording a string of No 1 hits for RCA Records. He was 22 years old at the time, and some of the alterations made during his two-decade residence in the house suggest he never lost his playful, boyish sense of grandeur. There's a jungle room with green shag carpeting on the ceiling, a swank TV room with three monitors (which Elvis is rumored to have enjoyed shooting at) and an immense, unsightly racquetball gym in the back yard, where hundreds of gold and platinum discs now hang above mannequins sporting the King's sequined threads from his flamboyant cape-donning days.

The upstairs rooms are off-limits, so we are denied a look at the famous toilet where the King reputedly met his maker. But since Elvis is buried on the grounds, in a prayer garden next to the swimming pool, we are able to pay respects in perhaps a more appropriate setting.

The Graceland experience can only be described as a confusion of admiration and bemusement. It's an odd privilege to freely scrutinize the man's personal effects in his own home. The tours inevitably draw a mix of diehard worshippers, casual fans, earnest sociology professors and the perversely curious. All are fully rewarded.

The 1½-hour mansion tour is a recording narrated by ex-wife Priscilla, with sound bites from Elvis and his daughter, Lisa Marie. Additional exhibits include Elvis memorabilia, an aircraft collection and a car museum, all with separate admission or included in the all-attractions package.

To get to Graceland from downtown, take I-55 south to Elvis Presley Blvd, and head south on that just a few blocks. On surface streets, you can take Union St to Bellevue and follow that south till it becomes Elvis Presley Blvd.

SUN STUDIO

☎ 901-521-0664, 800-441-6249; www.sunstudio.com; 706 Union Ave; admission $9.50; ⏰ 10am-6pm

Rock fans' number-one musical shrine is Sun Studio. It offers a simple, one-room, 30-minute tour that packs a punch because so many important events took place here during the 1950s. Some say rock and roll took its first flight in this tiny studio when Elvis Presley recorded his legendary 'Sun sessions' here in 1954. Others argue that rock began in 1951, when Jackie Brenston's 'Rocket 88' was recorded at Sun. (Of course, some would object to the notion that a single song gave birth to such a broadly defined musical category.)

Sam Phillips opened Sun in the early 1950s, initially concentrating on blues artists like Howlin' Wolf, BB King and Ike Turner. The impressive

↓ BLUES & BBQ MEMPHIS

catalog of blues sides recorded at Sun includes Rufus Thomas' 'Bear Cat,' Little Junior Parker's 'Mystery Train,' Howlin' Wolf's 'Highway Man,' Sleepy John Estes' 'Registration Day Blues,' James Cotton's 'Cotton Crop Blues,' and Little Milton's 'If You Love Me.'

After Elvis passed through, Sun cemented its place in rock history by churning out seminal recordings by Jerry Lee Lewis, Carl Perkins, Johnny Cash and Roy Orbison. The studio is still operational at night, favored naturally by artists seeking that unique Sun sound. During the day, guests can stand amid vintage instruments and recording gear and soak it all in. The label's blockbuster country and rockabilly cuts include Elvis Presley's 'That's All Right,' Jerry Lee Lewis' 'Great Balls of Fire' and 'Whole Lotta Shakin' Goin On,' Johnny Cash's 'I Walk the Line' and 'Folsom Prison Blues' and Carl Perkins' 'Blue Suede Shoes.'

STAX MUSEUM OF AMERICAN SOUL MUSIC

☎ 901-942-7685; www.staxmuseum.com; 926 E McLemore Ave; admission $9; ⏰ 10am-4pm Mon-Sat, 1-4pm Sun

This is an essential stop for anyone who remembers the old Stax logos – the wobbling platters on a record changer, the snapping fingers – and the great soul music that came out of Memphis during the '60s.

In 1960, Jim Stewart and Estelle Axton established Stax (the name contrived by mashing 'Stewart' and 'Axton' together) in an empty movie theater on E McLemore Ave. The studio assembled a mixed-race stable of artists, including Booker T Jones and Steve Cropper, that bucked segregationist tradition and shaped that distinctive Stax sound. Within a couple of years, the label was turning out hit records with regularity, giving Stax every right to claim the title 'Soulsville USA.'

Hits recorded at Stax include Wilson Pickett's 'In the Midnight Hour,' Otis Redding's 'Dock of the Bay,' Booker T & the MGs' 'Green Onions,' Carla Thomas' 'Gee Whiz,' Sam & Dave's 'Soul Man' and Isaac Hayes' 'By the Time I Get to Phoenix.'

If the Stax Museum fails to give visitors goose pimples, it's because the original building was demolished in 1989. The museum stands at the original address, however, and looks much the same, with a theater marquee emblazoned with the words 'Soulsville USA' and a small Satellite Records shop next to the entrance. It's worth visiting for the photos, displays of '60s and '70s peacock clothing and, above all, Isaac Hayes' 1972 Superfly Cadillac, outfitted with shag fur carpeting and 24k-gold exterior trim.

To get to Stax from downtown, follow 3rd St south to McLemore Ave and turn left. It's a few blocks to the east.

WC HANDY'S HOUSE

☎ 901-522-1555; 352 Beale St; admission $3; ⏰ 10am-5pm Tue-Sat

The Father of the Blues – so named in recognition of his being the first composer to publish a blues song, in 1909 – was born in Florence, Alabama, but moved first to Clarksdale, Mississippi, and then to Memphis to establish himself as a musician. William Christopher (WC) Handy occupied a humble shotgun house on Jennette St from about 1905 to 1918. During his time there he wrote 'Memphis Blues,' which originally was a campaign ditty for Boss Crump's first mayoral campaign, and 'Beale St Blues,' which put Memphis on the blues map. The tune for which Handy will always be remembered, however, is 'St Louis Blues.' The house was moved to Beale St and has been restored; it's filled with memorabilia recalling Handy's career. A knowledgeable tour guide adds value to the visit.

BEALE ST

The strip from 2nd to 4th Sts is filled with clubs, restaurants, souvenir shops and neon signs – a veritable theme park of the blues. It all refers back to Beale St's heyday, in the early 20th century, when the street was a cultural lightning rod for the African American community. Lined with shops and offices that catered to blacks, the street lit up at night when jazz clubs, blues joints and houses of ill repute yawned off the day's slumber.

Only one store is an original Beale St institution; the newer establishments offer up ersatz, and decidedly clean, representations of what the street must have looked like a century ago. It's easy and safe to walk around.

The original **A Schwab's** (☎ 907-523-9782; 163 Beale St; admission free; ☺ 9am-5pm Mon-Sat) dry-goods store has three floors of voodoo powders, 99-cent neckties, clerical collars and a big selection of hats.

The Smithsonian's **Rock 'n' Soul Museum** (☎ 901-543-0800; www.memphisrocknsoul.org; 145 Lt George W Lee Ave; admission $8.50; ☺ 10am-6pm) examines the social and cultural history that nurtured the music of Memphis and the Mississippi Delta. Next door (at the same address), the giant **Gibson Beale Street Showcase** (☎ 800-444-4766; admission $10; ☺ tours 1pm Sun-Wed, 11am, noon, 1pm & 2pm Thu-Sat) gives way-cool 30-minute tours of its guitar factory, where solid blocks of wood are transformed into those prized Gibson guitars.

At the heart of Beale St is **WC Handy Park**, a public space with a stage. Blues musicians have played in the park since it was dedicated in WC Handy's honor way back in 1931. These days, it's usually electric blues.

NATIONAL CIVIL RIGHTS MUSEUM

☎ 901-521-9699; www.civilrightsmuseum.org; 450 Mulberry St; admission $10; ☺ 9am-5pm Wed-Sat, 1-5pm Sun

From the street, the **Lorraine Motel**, where civil rights leader Martin Luther King Jr was fatally shot on April 4, 1968, appears eerily frozen in time. Two 1960s Cadillacs are parked in front and a memorial wreath hangs on the balcony in front of Room 6, where Dr King spent his last night. Inside, the hotel has been disemboweled and is now part of the monumental National Civil Rights Museum. King's room, however, has been preserved and carefully arranged to suggest nothing has been touched, from the unfinished breakfast to the rumpled sheets. The rest of the museum chronicles one of the most significant moments in modern American history. Documentary photos and audio displays chronicle key events in civil rights history.

FULL GOSPEL TABERNACLE
☎ 901-396-9192; 787 Hale Rd; ⊙ 11am Sun

These days the most soulful music in town is heard in this church, presided over by the Rev Al Green. Green, of course, is the extraordinary soul singer who reached No 1 on the pop and R&B charts in 1971 with 'Let's Stay Together.' After recording dozens of hit singles and some exemplary albums, Green left the pop music industry in 1980 and took up residence here. Green doesn't appear at the church every week, but even when he's away, the electric backup band and choir will blow the rug off your head if you're wearing one.

Visitors are welcome to attend the 2½-hour Sunday service at 11am. Etiquette tips for the uninitiated: Dress neatly, put at least $1 per adult in the collections tray, and don't leave early.

The church is in Whitehaven, near Graceland. Drive four traffic lights south of Graceland on Elvis Presley Blvd, and turn right at Hale Rd; it's a half-mile from there.

WDIA RADIO STATION
112 Union Ave

In 1949, WDIA (1060 on your AM dial) adopted an all-black format, something no other radio station in the US had done up to that time. The station's broadcasts of recorded music and live performances were beamed to a blues-hungry audience throughout western Tennessee and the upper Mississippi Delta. Through his slot on WDIA, advertising Pep-ti-kon tonic, BB King gained regionwide recognition that would lead to his becoming a major blues star. Rufus Thomas, a blues and novelty artist for Sun and Stax records, also hosted a show on WDIA. During its heyday, WDIA was broadcast from offices at 2267 Central Ave. Take a peek in the station's 3rd floor lobby to see some old photos on the wall, and snap some pics of your friends in front of the marquee out front.

SLEEPING

The big decision in Memphis is whether to stay near Graceland or downtown. The Graceland experience gets interesting when you approach it more intensely, so maybe one of the lodges on Elvis Presley Blvd is the way to go. On the other hand, there's lots to do downtown, and the atmosphere is a bit more real.

PEABODY HOTEL
☎ 901-529-4000, 800-732-2639; www.peabodymemphis.com; 149 Union Ave; r from $180; P ⊠

In the heart of the city, the landmark Peabody is Memphis' prize accommodation and a social hub, with a classy bar in its grand lobby. This is early-20th-century grandeur, with all the steamship amenities you might expect, plus it has ducks. Ducks? At 11am every day, the hotel's resident ducks are escorted from their penthouse apartment down to the lobby, where they have a swim in the marble fountain. They head back up to their quarters at 5pm sharp.

HEARTBREAK HOTEL
☎ 901-332-1000, 877-777-0606; www.heartbreakhotel.net; 3677 Elvis Presley Blvd; r $90-120; Ⓟ ⊠ ⊡

OK, so it's not at the end of Lonely St, but the Heartbreak Hotel, opposite Graceland, is all about Elvis. Elvis movies play in every room, and some of the biggest Presley fanatics stay here, so you'll be bumping into interesting people in the hall. The hotel offers a free shuttle to Beale St at night.

DAYS INN GRACELAND
☎ 901-346-5500; 3839 Elvis Presley Blvd; d $50-60; Ⓟ ⊠ ⊡

With its free Elvis movies and guitar-shaped pool, this chain bends over backwards to make Elvis fans at home. All that's missing is a poolside luau with Shelley Fabares. It's just a few blocks from Graceland.

MEMPHIS-GRACELAND CAMPGROUND
☎ 901-396-7125; 3691 Elvis Presley Blvd; campsites $22-27, cabins $33; ⊡

You can play horseshoes with fellow Elvis fans at this RV park. The cabins are a good deal, but you'll need a sleeping bag. It's across the street from Graceland, behind the Heartbreak Hotel.

SUPER 8 MOTEL DOWNTOWN MEMPHIS
☎ 901-948-9005; 340 W Illinois Ave; r $33-43; Ⓟ ⊠

It's a bit run down and in an isolated former military compound next to the Memphis-Arkansas Bridge, but downtown's just a mile away and the rooms are certainly adequate. Get coupons at the visitors center for the lowest price. To get here, follow Crump Blvd till it becomes I-55, and take exit 12C.

RED ROOF INN
☎ 901-526-1050; www.redroof.com; 42 S Camilla St; d $50-70; Ⓟ ⊠ ⊡

This generic chain is a clean and convenient option just a half-mile east of downtown. A complimentary continental breakfast is included.

EATING

Memphis far exceeds its quota of over-the-top, lip-smacking, finger-licking, astoundingly good barbecue establishments. If you're 'cued out (What!? Already?!), you'll happily discover that Memphis can sing more than one note.

COZY CORNER
☎ 901-527-9158; 745 N Parkway; dishes $5-10; ☺ 10:30am-7pm Tue-Sat

A nondescript and very friendly neighborhood barbecue joint, Cozy

Pulled Pork

Nothing excites Southern saliva glands quite like a craving for pulled barbecue pork butt. In Memphis, it's chopped up and served with a tomato-based barbecue sauce and a dollop of coleslaw in a cheap white bun. This is a variation on the pulled-pork sandwiches that are so popular in the Carolinas and elsewhere in the South. Once you've tried one, you'll agree it knocks the pants off a hamburger any day of the week. You can buy them at barbecue stands and even some gas stations throughout the region.

By the way, pork butt is not actually the bum of a swine. It's the upper shoulder. The key to good barbecue pork is the rub (seasoning mix) and the cooking technique (it's best when done slowly at a low temperature). Recipes vary from cook to cook, but the following rub will create a little taste of Southern heaven at home:

Pork Rub

4 tablespoons paprika
2 tablespoons salt
2 tablespoons coarsely ground black pepper
2 tablespoons cumin powder
3 tablespoons dark brown sugar

1 tablespoon dried oregano
1 tablespoon cayenne pepper
2 teaspoons dried sage
2 bay leaves, ground
1 teaspoon dry mustard

Mix spices together thoroughly. Rub this mixture onto the meat and let it sit overnight. Barbecue or roast the meat, keeping the temperature very low (under 200°F), for about 2 hours per pound of meat. Do not cover the meat. Keep a roasting pan beneath the rack to catch fat drippings, which you can use to baste the meat periodically (or use a baste of equal parts apple cider, vinegar and olive oil). Once the meat is cooked, let it cool before shredding it. Mix in barbecue sauce and slap that butt on some buns.

Corner is well worth the five-minute drive from downtown. Everything on the menu is capable of gratifying your barbecue urge – be it links, pulled pork, the unexpected game hen – but the dry ribs (see Charlie Vergo's, below) will make you weep tears of happiness. Good blues and jazz are piped in over the humble but tidy dining-room tables. This is as good as it gets.

CHARLIE VERGO'S RENDEZVOUS

☎ 901-523-2746; 53 S 2nd St; dishes $8-20; ⏱ 5-11pm Tue-Thu, noon-11pm Fri-Sat

Memphis' most famous rib joint is Charlie Vergo's, acclaimed for having introduced 'dry ribs' to the salivating public early in the last century. Dry ribs aren't typical barbecue. They're charcoal-broiled, with a Greek spice mix sprinkled on the meat, and there's no sweet sauce lathered on. When it comes to saying who does the best dry ribs, folks are torn between Vergo's and Cozy Corner (p 13), but this jumping joint is right downtown, on an alley off Union Ave. The service is friendly and the family atmosphere very upbeat.

PAYNE'S
☎ 901-942-7433; 1393 Elvis Presley Blvd; dishes $4-10; ☺ 11am-7pm Mon-Sat, to 9pm Fri

Another highly lauded barbecue joint is Payne's, down the road from Graceland. Pork shoulder sandwiches, topped with coleslaw, are the way to go here.

ARCADE
☎ 901-526-5757; 540 S Main St; dishes $5-8; ☺ 7am-3pm Sun-Thu, 7am-9pm Fri-Sat

Fans of filmmaker Jim Jarmusch will want to duck into this classic restaurant, where scenes from *Mystery Train* were filmed. The menu features standard short-order hash, along with some standout meatloaf and Southern-cooked vegetables (ie stewed in pork fat), but the main draw is the atmosphere. The Arcade opened in 1919 and by all appearances was redecorated in the '50s. It's still looking spiffy, despite tracks worn by coffee mugs on the Formica tabletops. Elvis is reputed to have come here to satiate his hankerings for fried peanut-butter-and-banana sandwiches, and from time to time these are still available on the list of specials if you want to try one for yourself.

AUTOMATIC SLIM'S TONGA CLUB
☎ 901-525-7948; 83 S 2nd St; lunch $8-14, dinner $17-27; ☺ 11am-2:30pm Mon-Fri, 5-10pm Mon-Thu, 5-11pm Fri-Sat

Memphians flock here for creative upscale dining in an artsy atmosphere. The food is a highfalutin Southern-Caribbean hybrid: jerked meats, voodoo seafood stew, green-market vegetables and Tonga martinis. This is a fun and stylish departure from the smoky, bluesy side of town.

BARKSDALE RESTAURANT
☎ 901-722-2193; 237 S Cooper St; dishes $5-12; ☺ 7am-6pm Mon-Fri, 7am-2pm Sat-Sun

Good, gut-busting Southern cooking is what the Barksdale specializes in. Breakfast, of course, is a doozy: omelettes, fresh biscuits, slabs of ham, grits and coffee. Lunchtime meat-and-three specials also pack a wallop: chops, country-fried steak, catfish, cooked vegetables, steaming cornbread, iced tea and slices of pie. This is a casual, family-oriented place where church ladies and blues aficionados mix comfortably. To get there, head east on Union Ave, past McLean, and turn right on Cooper; it's just a block down.

A&R BAR-B-QUE
☎ 901-774-7444; 1802 Elvis Presley Blvd; dishes $5-8; ☺ 11am-7pm Tue-Sat

Barbecue always tastes better in nondescript little dives like this one (with a grinning pig on the front). Pulled pork, wet or dry ribs, catfish, tamales and barbecue spaghetti anchor the menu. A&R is a mile or so north of Graceland.

DYER'S BURGERS

☎ 901-527-3937; 205 Beale St; dishes $3-7.50; ⏱ 10:30am-1am Sun-Thu, 10:30am-3am Fri-Sat

You knew this wasn't going to be a health-food guide, right? Dyer's, in the heart of the Beale St nightclub district, specializes in hamburgers deep fried in yesterday's flavorful cooking grease and served up on 'genuine Wonder Bread buns,' as the menu boasts. The fries are hand cut and delicious, the floats and shakes tops. You can also get chicken tenders or a bologna sandwich with homemade chili on it.

TOPS BAR-B-Q

☎ 901-725-7527; 1286 Union Ave; dishes $6-10; ⏱ 11am-10pm

With many locations, including this convenient one in Midtown, Tops has been a Memphis favorite for cheap barbecue since 1952.

ENTERTAINMENT

The clubs that made Beale St famous were long gone when the city decided to revive the historic entertainment strip. What exists now has a theme-park atmosphere. But why complain about a blues-infused block party? There's little going on elsewhere in town.

BB KING'S

☎ 901-524-5464; 143 Beale St

BB's anchors the Beale St scene. It typically has the strip's best live music, and there's usually no cover charge. Mr BB has his name on clubs across the USA now. Half a century ago, it would have been unimaginable for a black blues musician to enjoy such commercial success. BB is on the road year-round, hitting every town from Ft Lauderdale, Florida, to Anchorage, Alaska. He usually drops by his Memphis club for one or two nights a year.

MR HANDY'S BLUES HALL

☎ 901-528-0150; 182 Beale St

The most atmospheric club on Beale St has live blues every night. If the band's not rocking your world (a possibility), you can redirect your attention to some genuinely cool memorabilia and aged photos on the smoky brick walls. It's joined at the hip with the **Rum Boogie Cafe** (same address), another jumping joint.

WILD BILL'S LOUNGE
☎ 901-762-5473; 1580 Vollintine Ave

If you're looking for a friendly, authentic blues club, Wild Bill's fits the bill. This colorful little joint is in a middle-class African American neighborhood, and it serves locals well and makes out-of-town strangers feel welcome. The music is live on weekends, when the house band rattles the tables, and good recorded tunes stoke the room the rest of the week. Beer is served in 40oz bottles along with a classy drinking glass. Soul food is available here, too. To get there from downtown, take North Parkway to N Watkins and turn left; at Vollintine, turn right.

KUDZU CAFÉ
☎ 901-525-4924; 603 Monroe Ave

This is no blues club, but Kudzu does represent a welcome respite from touristy Beale St action. It's kind of a hippy-dippy Southern hangout, where comedians, singer-songwriters and guitar-pickers try out their material. Cheap beer, bar food and a convivial atmosphere make this a winner.

NEW DAISY THEATER
☎ 901-525-8979; www.newdaisy.com; 330 Beale St; shows at 7pm

This hip, all-ages venue hosts a variety of live music shows. Call the hotline to see what's playing.

MEMPHIS REDBIRDS
☎ 901-721-6000; tickets $5-17

The hometown nine are a Triple-A Minor League Baseball team, part of the St Louis Cardinals' farm system. They play frequent games before an enthusiastic crowd in their classy downtown yard, **Autozone Park** (N 3rd St & Union Ave). Minor League ball has its advantages, such as cheerleaders, live organ music, smaller parks (no bad seats) and laissez-faire fans.

ORPHEUM THEATER
☎ 901-743-2787; www.orpheum-memphis.com; 203 S Main St

This grand old vaudeville palace was built in 1928 and has been restored as a venue for Broadway shows and major concerts. From beneath the Orpheum's broad marquee, look across the street and you'll see a bronze statue of Elvis Presley.

SHOPPING

SHANGRI-LA RECORDS
☎ 901-274-1916; www.shangri.com; 1916 Madison Ave; ⊙ noon-7pm Mon-Fri, 11am-6pm Sat, noon-5pm Sun

Out in Mid-City, this record shop features a good selection of new and used CDs and LPs, with a Memphis emphasis. The store also has some fascinating music memorabilia on its walls.

SUN STUDIOS GIFT SHOP

☎ 901-521-0664, 800-441-6249; www.sunstudio.com; 706 Union Ave; admission $9.50; ☯ 10am-6pm

The little gift shop at Sun has a selection of T-shirts and concert posters reprinted from original '50s plates. Elvis, Johnny Cash and Howlin' Wolf are all well represented here.

ON THE ROAD

Getting out of Memphis and onto Hwy 61 is as easy as turning south on 3rd St, which doubles as Hwy 61. You'll pass through some gritty South Memphis neighborhoods before the cotton fields start to roll out before you.

Just over the Mississippi line, outside the tiny town of Walls, is **Memphis Minnie's Grave**. Born Lizzie Douglas in Algiers, Louisiana, she grew up in the northern Delta, made a name for herself on Beale St, began recording in 1929, and adopted a refined, urban style in Chicago. She was a rare female guitarist and much admired for her intricate finger-picking technique, powerful vocals and her worldly wise lyrics. To get to her grave, turn right on Hwy 302, left on Hwy 161, right on 2nd St, cross the tracks, veer right onto Old Hwy 61 (avoiding the decrepit dead-end), follow that 2 miles, and turn right on Norfolk Rd (at the 'Church' sign). A few hundred yards down the road you'll see the graveyard in front of the church. Minnie's monument is the big one in the middle, inscribed thusly: Lizzie 'Kid' Douglas Lawlers aka Memphis Minnie, June 3, 1897–Aug 6, 1973.

Continue down Hwy 61 to **Robinsonville**. Take Hwy 304 west 4 miles, and you'll reach the **Abbay & Leatherman Plantation**, where Robert Johnson grew up. Johnson learned guitar here from an old musician named Willie Brown, who was well respected in the area. Another of Johnson's early influences was Son House, who also lived and performed in Robinsonville. Charlie Patton and Howlin' Wolf also passed through the town in their itinerant wanderings. There's not much to see at the plantation, apart from cotton fields and an old office with a small 'Abbay & Leatherman' sign.

From here, Hwy 304 soon becomes Casino Strip Blvd, which leads to the **Horseshoe Casino** (☎ 800-363-7666). The gaudy casino itself is a jarring departure from our tour's theme, but a large room within it hosts the **Blues and Legends Hall of Fame Museum**, which has some great photos, old guitars and profiles of musicians from around the US and beyond.

To get to downtown Robinsonville, take Hwy 304 back toward Hwy 61 and head south on Old Hwy 61. In town, **Hollywood Cafe** (☎ 662-363-1126; 1585 Old Commerce Rd; ☯ open 6pm Thu-Sat) is a fun spot for dinner and dancing. You'll get some good catfish here and battered frog legs, too, if you're willing. Reservations are a good idea.

From Robinsonville, it's best to continue south on Old Hwy 61. This remnant of the old road is far more evocative of the way the Delta would have looked to the blues men who traveled from town to town in the pre-WWII years. Continue past little graveyards, fields and rusted farm equipment to **Tunica**. Its sleepy

DETOUR: NORTH TO CHICAGO

Chicago is a logical extension to a Hwy 61 blues tour. After all, the Windy City is where the blues ended up. Mississippi natives migrated to Chicago when mechanical cotton-pickers eliminated employment opportunities in the Delta. Many blues musicians followed their fan base and also moved to Chicago, where the music morphed into an electric, urban blues. Muddy Waters' band epitomized the shift, and Howlin' Wolf was Muddy's biggest rival in Chicago. Dozens of other blues legends made the same move, and most of them recorded for Chicago's Chess label.

Travelers who take the train from Memphis to Chicago can gain some satisfaction knowing that this was the same course followed by so many Mississippians decades ago. The chugging rhythm of the railroad resounds in many a blues classic.

Chicago is huge and worthy of several days' visit. For a thorough exploration, pick up Lonely Planet's *Chicago* city guide. Here we'll just provide a few blues highlights to wet your whistle.

Chicago has two noteworthy music festivals in June. Its **Blues Festival** is the biggest free blues fest in the world, and the **Gospel Festival** features a nonstop lineup of gut-wrenching performances by singers straining to please Him, with a capital H.

For sightseeing, head straight to **Willie Dixon's Blues Heaven** (☎ 312-808-1286; 2120 S Michigan Ave; admission $10; ⏰ 10am-4pm Mon-Fri, 11am-3pm Sat). In this humble building in the Near South Side, the Chess brothers started a recording studio in 1957 and set out to record a great number of blues musicians who had migrated north from Mississippi and elsewhere. Muddy Waters, Howlin' Wolf, Bo Diddley, Chuck Berry and many other blues legends cut tracks here. Now a museum, it holds a collection of blues memorabilia.

Chicago's nightlife is rife with blues action. **Buddy Guy's Legends** (☎ 312-427-0333; 754 S Wabash Ave) is run by the venerable Mr Guy himself. When the owner isn't playing, the joint still puts on the top blues acts.

Rosa's Lounge (☎ 773-342-0452; 3420 W Armitage Ave) is a hardcore blues club that draws top local talent and dedicated fans to a somewhat dodgy West Side block.

Blue Chicago (☎ 312-642-6261; 536 & 736 N Clark St) is a pair of friendly clubs on easily accessed downtown blocks.

Noisy, hot and sweaty, **B.L.U.E.S.** (☎ 773-528-1012; 2519 N Halsted St) and **Kingston Mines** (☎ 773-477-4646; 2548 N Halsted St) are conveniently located near el trains and keep it going till 4am.

Green Mill (☎ 773-878-5552; 4802 N Broadway) has a faded but no less sultry 1930s atmosphere, and top-notch jazz combos perform regularly. The place conjures images of Capone-era Chicago, and sure enough, this was one of Al's favorite watering holes.

Main St is a quaint throwback to the past, and **Nickson's Disco Club** (Magnolia St, off Main St; dishes $4-8) is a cool and atmospheric nightclub filled with friendly folks, red vinyl booths, a tin ceiling and a booming jukebox featuring solid blues and soul tunes. The kitchen here can straighten you out with some fried catfish or barbecue chicken, and a bottle of Bud will set you back a couple of bones. Next door, **Jack's Place** sometimes has live music. Also on Magnolia St, if you double back to the other side of Main St, stands a neat-looking **log cabin** that dates to 1840.

Blue and White (☎ 662-363-1371; 1355 Hwy 61N; dishes $5-11; ⏰ 6am-10pm), off the highway in Tunica, has been slingin' hash

The Wanderings of Robert Johnson

Robert Johnson, like a lot of Mississippi blues men from the early 20th century, was a rambler who left hazy recollections and a cloud of mythology in his wake. You're likely to sense his ghost at lonely crossroads throughout the Delta.

He was born in Hazlehurst, south of Jackson, on May 8, 1911. He lived in Memphis for a year or two when he was really young, before he and his mother settled in Robinsonville, Mississippi, where Johnson lived from about ages 7 to18. He began to play guitar in Robinsonville and met Charlie Patton and Son House there. Patton and House were far superior players, so Johnson left town.

When he returned to Robinsonville a year or so later, Johnson had dramatically refined his craft, and the intensity of his playing seemed to take the Delta blues into a new, supernatural realm. As the story goes, Johnson had gone off to sell his soul to the devil, in return for unprecedented skill as a blues man. Johnson encouraged the myth, but the likely truth is that he'd returned to Hazlehurst and practiced obsessively. Johnson also had familiarized himself with the varied styles of non-Delta players like Kokomo Arnold, Peetie Wheatstraw ('the devil's son-in-law') and Skip James. He absorbed their material, built upon the traditional Delta styles, and created something altogether new.

Johnson traveled widely throughout the Delta and the northeastern US, hopping trains and hitching rides as far as Michigan and New York with nothing but his guitar and the pin-striped suit on his back. In 1936, he went to San Antonio, Texas, to record his first sides, then went to Dallas the following year to record his last sides. These few recordings and a couple of photographs are the only concrete evidence of Johnson's brief flash as one of the greatest blues men to walk the earth.

During the 1930s, he lived on and off with a girlfriend in Helena, Arkansas, until his death in Greenwood, Mississippi, in 1938. The official death certificate implied Johnson died of syphilis, but the Johnson legend maintains that he was poisoned after making eyes at another man's woman. Even the whereabouts of his grave are disputed: you can pay your respects to the memory of Robert Johnson in three different graveyards. (See 'Where Lies Robert Johnson?' p42.)

Top Five Juke Joints
- **Poor Monkey Lounge** (p34), Merigold
- **Blue Front Cafe** (p47), Bentonia
- **Red's** (p32), Clarksdale
- **Ground Zero** (p32), Clarksdale
- **Vaughan's** (p60), New Orleans

since 1937. The great old joint can set you up with a full Southern breakfast (fresh biscuits, grits, eggs, ham, the works) or chicken dumplings or blue-plate specials and fresh vegetables (a rarity in these parts). The place is particularly festive after church on Sunday, when folks head straight here for the turkey and dressing.

Follow Old Hwy 61 a few miles south of Tunica and look out for the **Evansville Gen Store**, on the right, a rustic old market with a solitary gas pump that's worth a quick photo stop. The road widens a bit for **Lula**, a tiny town with a row of ancient brick shops, among them the **Washbucket**, a one-time laundry that now appears to be a place where old men gather to swap fish tales, and **Lula Gro Co** (dishes $6.50), where you can order a mess of ribs and potato salad to take out. On weekends, when folks are hanging out, Lula can be a friendly sort of place where the locals immediately peg you as a stranger and wonder about you.

South of Lula, the road turns into Lula–Moon Lake Rd, which leads to Hwy 49. Head west to go to Helena, or east to get back to Hwy 61 and Clarksdale. But if you simply head straight on Moon Lake Rd, you'll reach Moon Lake and **Uncle Henry's Place and Inn** (☎ 662-337-2757; www.unclehenrysplace.com; 5860 Moon Lake Rd; r $50-100; dishes $10-20; ☺ restaurant open 6pm Wed-Sun), a charming five-room B&B and restaurant. Long ago it was the Moon Lake Casino, and it is now one of the area's best spots for an upscale Creole dinner.

HELENA, AR

Population 6323; Map 3

Just across the Mississippi River Bridge on Hwy 49, this Arkansas town has seen better days. But its nearly deserted downtown streets – particularly Cherry St and Elm St – are visually fascinating, and a lot of history went down here. In the first half of the 20th century, Helena was a hub for African Americans, as there was plenty of work for black dockworkers. As tended to happen where there was disposable income, bootleggers, gamblers, prostitutes and entertainers gravitated to Helena in great numbers.

So Helena was a major port of call for blues men, and many hung their hats here on a regular basis. Robert Johnson shacked up with a girlfriend for half the 1930s in Helena. Her son was Robert Jr Lockwood, who learned many tricks on guitar from

Johnson. Robert Nighthawk, Roosevelt Sykes and Howlin' Wolf all lived in Helena for at least part of their lives. The crown prince of Helena, however, was Rice Miller, otherwise known as Sonny Boy Williamson II, who hosted his 'King Biscuit Time' radio program from Helena's KFFA radio station (see 'King Biscuit Time,' below). Little Walter Jacobs, a teenage runaway from Louisiana, lived in Helena for two or three years during the mid-'40s and studied Sonny Boy's style before heading up to Chicago, where he would revolutionize blues harmonica by amplifying the instrument. Little Walter also had a radio show on KFFA in the King Biscuit mold.

There are a lot of interesting sights to check out in Helena, enough to fill an afternoon, and there are some friendly bars and a couple of very nice accommodations, so you might even stay a night here.

Helena truly comes to life for the **King Biscuit Blues Festival** (www. kingbiscuitfest.org; admission free), when blues musicians and fans take over downtown for three days in early October. The music is just half the attraction; food stalls selling home-cooked soul food and barbecue are the other half.

SIGHTS

Most attractions in Helena are downtown, but you'll certainly want to drive out to take a few snaps of the King Biscuit Trailer. **Elm St** was the main drag for black businesses and once was lined by more than 40 taverns. In the old days, **Cherry St** was a similarly debauched strip for whites. Today, most of the rusticated brick buildings are still standing, but the city lacks the vitality it once had. Many of the buildings are vacant, their hand-painted signs fading away, and they're a comely sight in their state of gradual decay.

King Biscuit Time

Tall, droopy-eyed and snappily dressed, Sonny Boy Williamson II (Rice Miller) was one of the most entertaining and innovative blues harpists. He made a name for himself in 1941, when he began hosting 'King Biscuit Time' on Helena's KFFA 1360 AM. The noontime program ran just 15 minutes a day – beginning with the announcement, 'Pass the biscuits, 'cause it's King Biscuit Time' – and gave Sonny Boy and his partner, Robert Jr Lockwood, enough time to play a few tunes and plug upcoming live performances. The blues-and-biscuits combo proved so popular that the show's sponsor, King Biscuit Flour, put Sonny Boy's picture on its bags. And Sonny Boy's harp phrasings, packing the force and complexity of an entire horn section, influenced every harmonica player within the station's 80-mile radius.

King Biscuit Time (www.kingbiscuittime.com) still airs for half an hour Monday to Friday starting at 12:15pm. The show is hosted by Sunshine Sonny Payne, who has filled Sonny Boy's big shoes since 1951. (See Delta Cultural Center p23.)

KING BISCUIT TRAILER & KFFA RADIO
☎ **870-338-8361; 1360 Radio Dr**

It's worth driving the short distance out of town to see the rusty old King Biscuit Trailer, which has literally been put out to pasture near the KFFA radio towers. The trailer and its hand-painted sign – 'King Biscuit Flour, White...Dainty...Light' – are historically interesting chiefly for the trailer's connection to Sonny Boy Williamson II, whose radio program on KFFA helped advertise King Biscuit Flour. It's a surefire photo-op for Sonny Boy fans. KFFA's office is in a less picturesque trailer closer to the radio towers. KFFA's original location was downtown, on Walnut St. The station was also based at 302 Cherry St for many years, starting in 1960. 'King Biscuit Time,' however, is now broadcast from the Delta Cultural Center.

To get to the trailer, follow Hwy 49 toward West Helena; there's a traffic light at Hwy 242, where you'll turn right, and right again almost immediately onto Hwy 185. You'll spot the trailer just another half-mile down the road.

DELTA CULTURAL CENTER
☎ **870-338-4350; 141 Cherry St; $1 donation;** ☺ **10am-5pm Mon-Sat, 1-5pm Sun**

The modest exhibits here won't bring eyesight to the blind. The real attraction is the 'King Biscuit Time' radio program, which is broadcast from the center weekdays at 12:15pm. Visitors are warmly welcome to come watch Sunshine Sonny Payne announce the show.

SLEEPING

You'll need to reserve a room early for the King Biscuit Blues Festival, and you might even need to stay over the river in Tunica or Clarksdale. That said, Helena and nearby West Helena have some gorgeous old B&Bs.

EDWARDIAN INN
☎ **870-338-9155, 800-598-4749; www.edwardianinn.com; 317 Biscoe St; r $65-99;** ✗ ♺

This is a great old house, built in 1904 and immaculately restored. Rooms all have private baths and antiques. It's off Hwy 49B in West Helena.

MAGNOLIA HILLS
☎ **870-338-6874; 608 Perry St; r $65-95**

Just eight blocks from downtown, this Victorian B&B is a stunner. Its four rooms each have private baths and a sitting area, and the proprietors really pamper their guests. Breakfast is a winner.

DELTA INN
☎ **870-572-7915, 877-748-8802; 1207 Hwy 49N; r $45-65**

In West Helena, this motel is more than adequate at a very reasonable price.

EATING & ENTERTAINMENT

PASQUALE'S TAMALES
☎ 870-338-6722; 211 Missouri St; tamales $5/half-dozen; ⏱ 9am-5pm Mon-Fri

Historic Pasquale's is a local institution. Spicy beef tamales, the main attraction here, are popular throughout the Delta. Mexican laborers have long passed through the region, and this is the one delicacy of theirs that seems to have caught on. Pasquale's Sicilian owners make sure the menu always includes good pasta plates and New Orleans muffuletta sandwiches.

ROSIE'S
121 Missouri St

The longtime home of the late Frank Frost, a local blues man who kept the embers alive into the late 1990s, no longer offers live music. But it's a friendly little juke, where men often stand out front and invite you in for a drink.

FONZIE'S
400 Cherry St

The mirrored windows of Fonzie's, on the main drag, are kind of a turnoff. But the joint sometimes features live blues and jazz.

SHOPPING

BLUES CORNER
☎ 870-338-3501; 105 Cherry St

This little record shop, accessed through an antique store, has a mixed selection of blues, jazz, gospel and R&B CDs. There's also a modest selection of vinyl and some snazzy T-shirts. The store's worth a stop even if just to chat with the proprietor, Bubba Sullivan, who is a font of knowledge on regional blues.

GIST MUSIC COMPANY
☎ 870-338-8441; 307 Cherry St

The storefront of the Gist Music Company is pretty much what you'd expect a Delta music shop to look like – little has changed in about half a century apart from the addition of natural character wrought by time. Local blues musicians used to stop by here frequently to admire the latest guitars and harmonicas, and the proprietors often have enough time to share a few stories with visitors.

ON THE ROAD

Cross the bridge back over to Coahoma County, Mississippi, and head south down Hwy 1, a two-lane blacktop that follows the levee. Almost 15 miles down the road, you'll reach the tiny town of Stovall. Keep your eyes peeled for the Stovall Rd turnoff, and make a left. You'll soon be passing the fields of **Stovall Farms**, where Muddy Waters lived from age three to 30, prior to his move to Chicago.

Muddy's rough-hewn cabin no longer stands on the Stovall planta-tion, having been taken apart and reassembled at the Delta Blues Museum in Clarksdale. The Stovall house remains and is still lived in by descendants of Muddy's boss, Col William Howard Stovall. Continue down Stovall Rd to Clarksdale. The road becomes Oakhurst Ave as it enters town.

CLARKSDALE, MS

Population 20,645; Map 4

More than any other Delta town, Clarksdale celebrates its blues heritage, making this a good base for blues travelers. The Delta's northernmost town of any significant size, Clarksdale was a jumping-off point for blacks catching trains to Memphis or Chicago.

Many blues artists lived in Clarksdale or in the surrounding fields, most famously Muddy Waters, who lived and worked in Coahoma County for nearly three decades. John Lee Hooker was born just outside Clarksdale; Son House lived in nearby Lyon; and Ike Turner, a Clarksdale native, hosted a radio show on WROX. Gospel-soul singer Sam Cooke was born and raised here. WC Handy spent two years in town, soaking up the blues that he would incorporate into his sophisticated jazz compositions, and Bessie Smith died in a hospital in Clarksdale.

Clarksdale's color line is demarcated by the railroad tracks. Downtown stands on one side, where the tracks meet the Sunflower

Visiting Juke Joints

It's believed that 'juke' is a West African word that survived in the Gullah Creole-English hybrid spoken by isolated African Americans in the US. The Gullah 'juke' means 'wicked and disorderly.' Little wonder, then, that the term was applied to roadside sweatboxes of the Mississippi Delta, where secular music, suggestive dancing, drinking and, in some cases, prostitution were the norm. The term 'jukebox' came into vogue when recorded music, spun on automated record-changing machines, began to supplant live musicians in such places, as well as in cafes and bars.

Most juke joints are black neighborhood clubs, and outside visitors can be a rarity. Many are mostly male hangouts; others are frequented by men and couples. There are very few places that local women, even in a group of two or three, would turn up without a male chaperone. Otherwise, women can expect a lot of persistent, suggestive attention.

For visitors of both sexes, having a friendly local with you to make some introductions can make for a much better evening. It can also help to call ahead to find out what's going on and to say you're going to stop by. If you arrive alone and unannounced, talk to people to break the ice – but women might want to act like they're training to be nuns.

Note that juke joints don't always keep regular hours. Some open only when the owner's in the mood (another reason to call ahead).

River, while African American residences and businesses have traditionally been on the other side, in the **New World District**. With Issaquena Ave and 4th St at its crux, the New World District was a wild, rip-snorting precinct lined with brothels, bars and legitimate shops, and blues musicians played the sidewalks and watering holes day and night. These days, the area is not just rough looking; it looks downright abandoned, although people often hang out in front of the boarded-up shops. There are still a few good jukes in the area.

At the town's south side, Hwys 61 and 49 meet at what locals refer to as the **crossroads**. You can't miss the large tin guitars that mark the spot. Does this busy intersection look like a good place to sell your soul to the devil? Some locals will have you believe Robert Johnson did just that, right here.

SIGHTS & ACTIVITIES

DELTA BLUES MUSEUM
☎ 601-627-6820; www.deltabluesmuseum.org; 1 Blues Alley; admission $6; ⏰ 9am-5pm Mon-Sat

The old train station that now houses the Delta Blues Museum was a freight depot for the Yazoo and Mississippi River Valley Railroad and the Illinois Central. It's big and filled with blues arcana, old photos and blues-inspired art. Star items include Muddy Waters' old cabin, in which he made his first recordings for Alan Lomax, and the sign from the demolished Three Forks store, where Robert Johnson is believed to have been poisoned. The museum also features traveling exhibits. You can get maps and charts that plot musical milestones, see a statue of Muddy Waters and peruse a modest collection of artifacts.

RIVERSIDE HOTEL
☎ 662-624-9163; 615 Sunflower Ave

This unremarkable-looking hotel is a blues landmark because in 1937, when it was the **FT Thomas Afro-American Hospital**, singer Bessie Smith

The Empress' Deathbed

On September 26, 1937, jazz singer Bessie Smith (born in 1894) was injured in a car accident on Hwy 61 as she entered Clarksdale. Bleeding profusely, she was brought in an ambulance to the Riverside Hotel, which then was a black medical clinic, and there she died. A popular legend has it that she was sent here after being refused at the whites-only hospital, but this is now considered to be untrue.

A native of Chattanooga, Tennessee, Smith was the highest-paid African American entertainer of the 1920s. She recorded 156 songs, including 'T'aint Nobody's Business If I Do,' WC Handy's 'St Louis Blues' and the brilliant 'Nobody Knows You When You're Down and Out.' Her singing style influenced Billie Holiday, Mahalia Jackson and Janis Joplin.

Blues Festivals

- **Juke Joint Festival**, Clarksdale, mid-April
- **Baton Rouge Blues Week**, Baton Rouge, late April
- **New Orleans Jazz & Heritage Festival**, New Orleans, late April– early May
- **Mississippi Delta Blues & Heritage Festival**, Greenville, mid-May
- **Crossroads Blues Festival**, Rosedale, May
- **BB King Hometown Homecoming**, Indianola, early June
- **Hwy 61 Blues Festival**, Leland, mid-June
- **Sunflower River Blues and Gospel Festival**, Clarksdale, early August
- **King Biscuit Blues Festival**, Helena, early October

died here after being injured in a car accident on Hwy 61 (see 'The Empress' Deathbed' p26). The hospital became a hotel in 1944, and blues musicians stayed here often, some on a semipermanent basis. Ike Turner lived at the Riverside Hotel when he was young, and Helena-based Sonny Boy Williamson II is known to have stayed here frequently after missing the last ferry over the river. The hotel's owner, Frank 'Rat' Ratliff, grew up in the hotel when it was run by his mother, the late Mrs ZL Hill, and he has many stories to tell. Ask to see Room 2, the Bessie Smith Room, which is fully made up to accommodate guests. A large poster of the singer tops the bed; her image looks eerily ghostlike in the dimly lit room. The front living room is filled with family photos, along with some unexpected snaps taken when John F Kennedy Jr stayed a night here in 1991.

WADE WALTON'S BARBERSHOP
317 Issaquena Ave

Sadly, you can no longer get your hair cut here, as the town's legendary barber, Wade Walton, passed on in 2000. However, his old shop still stands, just 'round the corner from the Blues Museum, with a pair of barbecue smokers parked out front. The dapper Walton was a local character and an accomplished musician. He was also known for his innovative barber-strop rhythms, performed while sharpening a razor. For many decades, blues musicians dropped by for a snip, including Howlin' Wolf and Sonny Boy Williamson II. Plans are afoot to turn the shop into a simple museum of sorts. Stay tuned...

The adjacent lot, long vacant, was the site of **WC Handy's Clarksdale residence**. Handy lived here from 1903–05. A plaque commemorates the man.

IKE TURNER'S HOME
304 Washington St

Tina Turner's ex grew up in Clarksdale and hosted a radio show on WROX, before moving up to Memphis, where he played a key role in the development of rock and roll. His poor singing voice kept him

Muddy Waters

Coahoma County's Muddy Waters was one of the blues' great innovators and an ambassador who introduced the music to new audiences around the world. He was born McKinley Morganfield on April 4, 1913, on a farm near Rolling Fork, but his family had settled on Stovall Farms by the time he was three. He would stay put for 27 years.

At Stovall, Muddy drove a 1934 Ford truck, which set him apart from mule-driving farmers. He also bootlegged whiskey and ran regular house parties out of his grandmother's cabin. He performed country blues at these parties, and word spread that he was a blues man to be reckoned with. John and Alan Lomax, traveling the Delta in search of music to record for their now legendary Library of Congress collection, heard about Muddy, and in 1941 and 1942, Muddy cut his first sides with them. A year later he left for Chicago.

In big-city taverns, acoustic blues were easily drowned out by noisy patrons, passing El trains and street traffic, so Muddy did what a lot of jazz players were doing and got himself an electric guitar. In the early '50s, he assembled a top-notch band, including Jimmy Rogers on guitar and Little Walter on harp, and together they took urban blues into entirely new territory. For five years, Muddy enjoyed unprecedented success for a blues artist, recording big hits with 'Hoochie Coochie Man,' 'I Just Want to Make Love to You,' 'Got My Mojo Workin',' and 'Mannish Boy.'

During the late '50s, he toured England, where he jumpstarted the British blues craze that would inspire the Rolling Stones (so named after a Waters song), the Animals, Eric Clapton, Led Zeppelin and countless other Blighty rockers. Muddy Waters died on April 30, 1983, in a suburb of Chicago.

from becoming a major star on his own, but he was known as much for spotting talent and directing it. He hit pay dirt with his singing pal Jackie Brenston, whose seminal 'Rocket 88' was recorded under Ike's musical direction (and with Ike's band) at Sun Studios. Ike's reputation rose with the success of Ike and Tina, but plummeted in the film *What's Love Got to Do with It?*, in which Laurence Fishburne gave a superb and menacing performance. Ike wasn't always the most likeable guy, but he sure could rock. To get to the house, take State St west of the river, then turn right on Washington. It's a couple of blocks up.

SUNFLOWER RIVER BLUES AND GOSPEL FESTIVAL
☎ 662-627-6805; www.sunflowerfest.org; free

Clarksdale's big blues festival takes place the first weekend in August, a hot and sweaty time of year. A big stage is set up on Blues Alley, and the emphasis here is traditional Delta-style blues. You'll see much more acoustic playing than at the other big fests, and because of the heat the crowds aren't as big. Barbecue stands line the street, and the local jukes jump at night.

JUKE JOINT FESTIVAL
☎ 662-627-4593; www.jukejointfestival.com; free

Expect blues, barbecue and pig racing on the streets of downtown Clarksdale. By night, the clubs jump. This fest takes place in mild mid-April.

SLEEPING

SHACK UP INN
☎ 662-624-8329; www.shackupinn.com; r $50-75; Ⓟ 🔀

At Hopson Plantation, 2 miles south on the west side of Hwy 49, the Shack Up offers much more than a place to lay your head. A night or two in one of the Shack Up's refurbished sharecropper cabins offers a totally unique experience that'll immerse you in Delta life. The cabins all have covered porches and are filled with old furniture and musical instruments. The more expensive ones sleep up to four people. The old commissary is an atmospheric venue for frequent live music performances, and the owners are fonts of information. Staying here is sure to be a highlight of your trip through the Mississippi Delta.

BELLE CLARK BED & BREAKFAST
☎ 662-627-1280; www.belleclark.com; 211 Clark St; r $125-195; Ⓟ ✕ 🔀

The home of John Clark, founder of Clarksdale, was built in 1859 and is now a gorgeous B&B. Antique-filled rooms and parlors are designed to evoke antebellum splendor and Tennessee Williams-style decadence. Williams, after all, grew up in the neighborhood (it's a posh Clarksdale enclave). It's not very bluesy but certainly is a treat. Most rooms have private baths.

UPTOWN MOTOR INN
☎ 662-627-3251; 305 E 2nd St; r $30; Ⓟ 🔀

Recently updated rooms, with refrigerators and microwave ovens, make this central motel a great value. Most Clarksdale sights are within blocks from here. None of the rooms is nonsmoking, so if that's a problem, you should do an air-quality check in the room before paying.

RIVERSIDE HOTEL
☎ 662-624-9163; 615 Sunflower Ave; r $30; 🔀

This is an authentic, historic blues site, and staying a night here will surely be an unforgettable part of your trip. There just weren't many Mississippi hotels that accommodated black blues men during the 1940s and '50s, and this is the only one still operating. So if you want to stay where Sonny Boy and others hung their hats, this is the place. The chatty owner, Frank Ratliff, runs a pretty tight ship. Rooms are small but clean and comfortable, and the bathroom is down the hall. Some rooms are occupied by semipermanent residents.

EATING

ABE'S BAR-B-QUE
☎ 662-624-9947; 616 State St; dishes $3-6; ☻ 10:30am-2pm Sun, 10am-9pm Mon-Thu, 10am-10pm Fri-Sat

At the crossroads, look for the tall sign with the happy pig in a bow tie. Abe's has been providing Clarksdale with zesty pork sandwiches on cheap white buns since 1924.

DELTA AMUSEMENT BLUES CAFÉ
☎ 662-627-1467; 348 Delta Ave; dishes $3-8; ☻ 8am-2pm Mon-Sat

A downtown favorite, Delta Amusement slings some sturdy hash for breakfast and lunch. The 'Big Plate' lunch specials ($7) are a feast and a bargain – we're talking tasty soul food. During festivals, the place moonlights as a juke, and sometimes late Saturday afternoons a jam session gets going.

MADIDI
☎ 662-627-7770; www.madidires.com; 164 Delta Ave; dishes $20-33; ☻ from 6pm Tue-Sat

Actor Morgan Freeman hails from the Clarksdale area and still lives nearby. Having decided the area needed a restaurant to satisfy his refined tastes, he opened Madidi with a local businessman. The food is French with a Mediterranean flair, and the atmosphere reserved but pleasant. Reservations recommended.

CHAMOUN'S REST HAVEN
☎ 662-624-8601; 419 State St; ☻ 5:30am-9pm Mon-Sat

The friendly Chamoun family are Lebanese-Americans who own the hospitable Rest Haven. It looks like an all-American coffee shop, with leatherette booths and Formica tabletops, and the menu features familiar fare like fried chicken, with Middle Eastern sides like dolmas and hummus. The pie is legendary.

HICK'S
☎ 662-624-9887; 305 State St; dishes $2-6; ☻ 11am-7pm Tue-Sat

This takeaway joint's locally famous for its Delta-style hot tamales, which are much skinnier than traditional Mexican tamales but equally tasty. You can also get wonderful barbecue here.

RANCHERO
☎ 662-624-9768; 1907 State St; dishes $5-15; ☻ 10am-10pm Mon-Thu, 10am-11pm Fri-Sat

'The Ranch' is family owned and well loved by the locals. It's known for its barbecue ribs and its homemade pies, and both are indeed special, as are the fried-fish plates.

OSCAR'S TAMALES
Cnr Yazoo Ave & Martin Luther King Blvd; tamales $1; ☻ noon-10pm Fri-Sat

From the back of a pickup truck parked at the corner of Yazoo Ave

There's also a mural of Sonny Boy Williamson II, who is buried in Tutwiler. To get to **Sonny Boy Williamson's gravesite**, follow 2nd St out of town, turn right on Bruister Rd, and follow it for a bit more than a mile. A small cemetery is on the right side of the road. Sonny Boy's grave is the tall granite monument toward the back, with a photo of the harp-blowing blues man. Many who visit the gravesite leave harmonicas as a fitting tribute. If you don't have a harp handy, Sonny Boy probably wouldn't object to a hip-flask filled with bourbon.

At Tutwiler, Hwy 49 splits into east and west branches, with Hwy 49W heading towards **Parchman Penitentiary**, the notorious prison farm that turns up in blues songs and Mississippi lore. Son House is reputed to have done two years' time here, as is Bukka White, who wrote and recorded songs about it after his release. The white blues pianist Mose Allison also wrote a catchy ditty called 'Parchman Farm.' Parchman is perhaps best known for the prison songs recorded by John and Alan Lomax for the Library of Congress. The prison is still in full operation, and merely a drive-by site on your way elsewhere. Hwy 32 heads from Parchman back to Hwy 61.

Shelby, on Hwy 61, has a few jukes, including **The Do Drop Inn** (Lake St), which features 'Ma Rene's home cooked bar-BQ' and live music on Sunday night.

From Shelby, Hwy 161 meanders down to **Merigold**, a sleepy little hamlet that weeds and vines appear ready to reclaim. A solitary yellow traffic light swings over the highway, indicating it's time to turn right and creep into the center of town. The ghostly downtown seems to have made an art of its own graceful decay and it's worthy of a few snapshots. Charlie Patton lived in Merigold from 1924–29. **Crawdad's** (☎ 662-748-2441; 104 S Park St; dishes $6-20; ☷ 6am-10pm Tue-Sat) is a massive, barnlike restaurant that serves Cajun cuisine, crawfish and steaks.

Mound Bayou

On Hwy 61, south of Shelby, the historic community of Mound Bayou was founded by freed slaves in 1887. Isaiah T Montgomery and Benjamin T Green, having purchased 840 acres, founded the town and named it after a Native American mound on the site. With a group of settlers, they cut the forests, sold timber, filled bayous and built log cabins. It was a difficult beginning, but Montgomery spurred on the settlers: 'You have for centuries hewed down forests at the request of a master. Could you not do it for yourselves and your children into successive generations that they may worship and develop under your own vine and fig tree?'

Mound Bayou grew in the early 20th century to a town of 4000 people. It was governed by blacks and had a self-sustaining economy. It's a pretty sleepy little town nowadays, but the National Park Service has designated the town a National Historic Site.

You've probably been dreaming about a ramshackle juke down a dirt road, the sounds of blues riffs and clinking bottles drifting out over the cotton fields. Just outside Merigold, **Poor Monkey Lounge** (☎ 601-748-2254; cover $3) fits the bill. This crazy little joint doesn't have live music, but DJ Candy Man spins blues here on Thursday night, and though it's a house-party atmosphere, conspicuous strangers are always welcome to join the action (just don't expect to be left alone). To get there, follow South St west of Hwy 61, take the immediate left at the fork, onto the unpaved road alongside a creek, and drive for more than a mile. You can't miss the tumble-down agglomeration of corrugated tin and wood paneling with illegible lists of rules hand-painted on the front.

CLEVELAND, MS

Population 13,840

This old sawmill town was once a rough-and-ready magnet for blues artists, and you can still see live music here. Delta State University, with some 4000 students, makes its home here. The downtown is pleasant, with antique and curio stores, and the town offers some solid eating and sleeping options. Cleveland is a good base if you're planning to hit the jukes of the central Delta.

SIGHTS

MISSISSIPPI DELTA BLUES HALL OF FAME
5th Ave at Court St

This sounds like more than it is. In the Charles W Capps Archives and Museum on the Delta State University campus, monumental plaques commemorate blues men honored in Cleveland's annual Peavine Awards. Inductees thus far (the Peavine Awards began only in 1998) include Charlie Patton, Willie Brown, Tommy Johnson, Robert Johnson, Robert Jr Lockwood, Henry Townsend, Son House, Muddy Waters, Little Milton, Robert Nighthawk, Houston Stackhouse, Joe Willie Wilkins, Bukka White, Howlin' Wolf and Ike Turner. The goal is to eventually build a permanent home for a full-fledged museum, but thus far the Peavine Awards has devoted its fundraising energies to helping student musicians.

The **Peavine Awards** take place in September or October each year and include a concert by a living legend. Call ☎ 662-846-4626 for ticket information.

SLEEPING

MOLLY'S BED & BREAKFAST
☎ 662-843-9913; www.shaman.home.dixie-net.com; 214 S Bolivar Ave; r $70

Molly Shaman's unusual B&B is the best place to stay in the central Delta. Her husband Floyd's quirky wood sculptures fill the themed rooms (Watermelon Room, Cowboy Room and so forth). It's in a wonderful old Victorian house, fully restored, and guests are treated to a full Southern breakfast.

DELTA INN
☎ 662-846-1873; 1139 Hwy 61S; r $30 & up

Here's a basic cheapie that'll do the trick if you're looking for bottom-end rates.

COLONIAL INN
☎ 662-843-3641; fax 662-252-5002; Hwy 61N; r $30-50

Slightly bigger, and a step up from the Delta Inn, this hotel is a pretty good value.

BEST WESTERN
☎ 662-846-5404, 800-528-1234; 900 S Davis Ave/Hwy 61S; r $52-66; P ⊠ ⟁

This chain goes beyond the call of duty with its good continental breakfast, swimming pool, workout room and laundry. It also includes the Highway 61 Blues Café, with a full bar.

EATING & ENTERTAINMENT

AIRPORT GROCERY
☎ 662-843-4817; Hwy 8W; dishes $6-16; ⊗ 11am-9:30pm Mon-Sat

Bookings are irregular, but this is where you're most likely to catch some live blues in Cleveland. Otherwise it's a casual restaurant that's reliable for barbecue, tamales, steaks and crawfish. Recorded blues are usually piped in. It's right on Hwy 8, as you're heading west out of town.

THE PIG PEN
☎ 662-843-0512; 419 S Davis Ave; dishes $5-10; ⊗ 10am-9pm Mon-Sat

Good people are running this great little cinderblock shack that ladles out tasty barbecue. It's along Hwy 61 south of town.

THE SOUTHERN GRILL
☎ 662-843-1317; 120 North St; dishes $3-9; ⊗ 6am-2pm

With fine food and fine people, this spot makes a good stop for a Southern breakfast or a meat-and-three lunch.

BEAN COUNTER
☎ 662-846-5282; 219 S Court St; ⊗ 7am-6pm Mon-Fri, 8am-4pm Sat

A rarity in the Delta, this is a coffeehouse that serves high-octane espresso drinks. You can also get light snacks here.

ON THE ROAD

Highway 61 is the main route through the Delta, but it doesn't hit all the spots and isn't always the most scenic route. From Cleveland, take narrow Hwy 8 west to the Mississippi River, where Hwy 1 nudges the levee. At the crossroads of Hwys 8 and 1, **Rosedale** is a

DETOUR: DOCKERY FARM

A regular stop on Delta blues pilgrimages is Dockery Farm, about midway between Cleveland and Ruleville along Hwy 8. A big photogenic cotton gin, visible from the highway, has a large sign painted on one side:

DOCKERY FARMS
EST 1895 BY
WILL DOCKERY 1865–1936
JOE RICE DOCKERY
1906–1982

This is where Charlie Patton lived on and off for about 30 years. Patton, often referred to as the 'King of the Delta Blues' and sometimes over-simply credited with *inventing* the blues, grew up on the farm after his sharecropper parents moved the family here in the mid-1890s. He began to play guitar before blues was a known musical form, then latched onto one of the first blues men to make a name for himself, Henry Sloan. By World War I, Dockery and the surrounding towns had gained a reputation for having a concentration of blues talents, so in Sloan, Patton probably had the best mentor available. He learned all of Sloan's tricks and quickly became the hottest blues performer in the Delta.

Patton began recording in 1929, several years past his prime, but his recordings are by turns haunted and frenetic and always powerful. He died in 1934. Patton's influence was widely felt during the pre–World War II years. Tommy Johnson, who lived just south of Cleveland, idolized Patton. Howlin' Wolf lived on the Dockery Plantation and learned from Patton as well. Roebuck 'Pops' Staples, of the gospel-singing family, grew up on Dockery and as a youngster was inspired by Patton. Robert Johnson knew Patton and emulated his guitar playing some before gravitating toward the style of Son House.

riverside town mentioned in Robert Johnson's 'Traveling Riverside Blues.' The town was known for its levee camps, where riverboat men and traveling musicians often gathered, and bootleggers are known to have done steady business here. In May, the modest **Crossroads Blues Festival** takes place here. Call Leo McGee at the **River Run Cafe** (☎ 662-759-6800; 1310 S Main St) for information. The **White Front Cafe** (☎ 662-759-3842; Main St; dishes $2.50 & up; ⊙ 9am-7pm) is a great little tamale joint in town. **Bug's Place** is a juke joint on Bruce St, which was Rosedale's swinging strip during the town's heady midcentury heyday. Blues comes out of the jukebox, but the joint's pretty lively and fun.

Great River Rd State Park (☎ 662-759-6762; www.mdwfp.com; campsites $9) is just over the levee from Rosedale and has wooded campsites and a whiskey still to commemorate the levee's raucous history. **Perry Martin Lake**, in the park, is named for a 1930s bootlegger who lived on a houseboat here. Martin kept his still in the woods nearby.

Continue meandering down rustic Hwy 1 to Greenville, along the way passing little bulges in the road like Beulah, Benoit and Lamont.

GREENVILLE, MS

Population 41,633

The Delta's largest city, Greenville is roughly midway between Clarksdale and Vicksburg. It was here that the levee broke during the catastrophic Great Flood of 1927. Until recently, **Nelson St**, the main drag in black Greenville, was one of the Delta's liveliest streets for juke joints and live music, but of late things have quieted down considerably. Nelson St has also long been notoriously crime-ridden, and although it's true that drugs and sex are bought and sold along the street, it's generally safe enough in the afternoon to drive or walk through to have a look at the dilapidated remains of the old district.

Otherwise there's little to see in Greenville. You'll find good food here, though, and this is one of the few Delta towns in which you'll find decent lodging.

On the third weekend in May, Greenville picks up for the **Mississippi Delta Blues & Heritage Festival** (☎ 662-335-3523; www.deltablues.org). The festival takes place in a cotton field off Hwy 454, south of town. Blues Week is a weeklong buildup preceding the festival. There are stages on Nelson St and bands perform in some of the bars. It's a good time to swing through Greenville.

SLEEPING

In addition to these options, there are numerous chain motels along Hwy 82E.

GREENVILLE INN & SUITES
☎ 662-332-6900; 211 Walnut St; r from $50; Ⓟ ⌧

In the old levee board building, this hotel has clean rooms and a very atmospheric riverside location. Walnut St restaurants are within a block.

LINDEN ON THE LAKE
☎ 662-839-2181; Lake Washington; r $85

This B&B is an old plantation home amid ancient live oak and magnolia trees, and it's still owned by the original family. Rooms in the house have antique furnishings, while cabins on the grounds are a bit more rustic. It's on Lake Washington, 22 miles south of Greenville, and the owners will lend you fishing gear. To get there, take Hwy 1 to Hwy 436, head west to the lake, then drive half a mile north to the house.

LEVEE INN

☎ 662-332-1511; 1202 Hwy 82E; r $29; Ⓟ ⌧

This medium-size hotel is an acceptable and cheap place to lay your head. It offers free HBO and local calls.

EATING & ENTERTAINMENT

DOE'S EAT PLACE

☎ 601-334-3315; 502 Nelson St; steaks $29 & up; ⌚ 5-9pm Mon-Sat

Doe's, going strong since 1941, hardly stands out on rough-and-tumble Nelson St, but it's known far and wide as one of the best steak houses in the Delta. Steaks and fries are exorbitantly expensive but huge enough (starting at 2lb) for two large adults to share. Doe's is also well loved for its tamales ($1), which can be ordered to go during the day. Suited folks from around town and tourists don't seem too worried about coming to Nelson St when they've got Doe's in mind.

BUD'S CAFE

☎ 662-378-8654; 1718 Old Leland Rd; dishes $5; ⌚ noon-2pm Mon-Sat

Now here's your basic soul food shack. It doesn't look like much, which of course is always a good omen, as is the fact that working folks, mostly black, love this place. Plates piled high with meat, peas and other good things live up to the non-hype.

JIM'S CAFÉ

☎ 662-332-5951; 314 Washington Ave; dishes $4-8; ⌚ 5am-7pm Mon-Sat

This is a classic eatery that's been in business for more than half a century. Older white folks make a regular habit of stopping by.

THE MEETING PLACE

☎ 662-335-9123; 247 S 6th St; dishes $2-5

The mural painted on the side of this juke, which is somewhat removed from Nelson St, tells you all you need to know: People dance here, play music here, have a good time here. It mostly serves the neighborhood, but outsiders who don't mind drinking from a 30oz bottle of Colt 45 will fit right in. Sunday evening is blues night. You can also order burgers, catfish, pork chops or chitlins here for very little money.

ON THE ROAD

East of Greenville, Hwy 82 heads out to Indianola, Greenwood and out of the Delta. But first, you'll reach the pretty little town of **Leland**, which has a rich blues heritage. The **Hwy 61 Blues Museum** (☎ 662-686-7646; cnr Broad & 4th Sts; admission $5; ⌚ 10am-4pm Mon-Sat), in the Old Temple Theater, honors local blues men Little Milton, Eddie Foster, Indianola's BB King and others. There are also some interesting **murals** in Leland. One on 3rd St between Broad and Main Sts depicts BB King as a young man, in middle age and as an elder statesman of the blues, riffing in front of tour buses. Around the block on 4th St, a mural celebrates blues artists born in or near Leland, including Little Milton, Jimmy Reed and the specter-like white blues men Johnny and Edgar Winter. This mural was painted in 2000, and some of the surviving musicians signed the wall next to it. Leland hosts the **Hwy 61 Blues Festival** in mid-June, usually starring Leland's own Eddie Cusic.

Leland is actually best known as the hometown of Muppet maestro Jim Henson. The town makes a little hoopla over the connection, with a small **Muppet exhibit** at the visitors center, along Hwy 82, and a sign on the Broad St bridge over Deer Creek identifying the spot as the 'birthplace of Kermit the Frog.' Kermit, of course, is known as a singer of the 'greens,' rather than the blues. The melancholy 'It's Not Easy Being Green' was his biggest hit.

Holly Ridge, up the highway from Leland, is where **Charlie Patton's grave** stands in a humble cemetery next to a cotton gin and some railroad tracks. Patton's modern headstone stands out, as it is crisply cut and one of the few to stand upright. Patton, described as 'the voice of the Delta' on his grave, lived the last two years of his life in this town. To get there, take the Holly Ridge turnoff from Hwy 82, drive a mile to Main St, turn left, and drive another half-mile, passing some modest homes, until you reach a huge cotton gin and graveyard on the left.

INDIANOLA, MS

Population 12,066

BB King's hometown: If a town's going to have only one real claim to fame, that's not a bad one at all. Riley 'BB' King was born September 16, 1925, outside Itta Bena, between Indianola and Greenwood. He moved to Indianola at the age of 13. He's still going strong, but he spends very little time in Indianola these days.

Hwy 82 runs right into Indianola, and motorists entering the town are greeted by a huge sign that says, 'Welcome to Indianola, Home of BB King.' You have to turn off this busy thoroughfare to see the actual town, though. Take Catching St south a few blocks into the old downtown, with its antiquated shop fronts and oblique angled grid. Cross the railroad tracks to reach the black part of town, with Church St at its center.

Blues guitarist Albert King, who is no relation to BB, is known to have grown up in Arkansas, but he was born in Indianola in 1923. Charlie Patton reportedly died here.

SIGHTS & ACTIVITIES

The corner of Church and 2nd Sts was young **BB King's favorite busking spot**. In the early 1940s, he would set up here on Saturday afternoon and play for change. 'On my corner both the blacks and whites would see me,' BB has said. 'It wasn't something I planned.

It was just like a good fishing place.' A plaque has been raised on the corner to commemorate its history, and a large, glass-covered photo of BB adorns the wall overlooking the spot. In 1986, BB returned to leave an impression of his footprints in some newly poured concrete on the corner, but they are already fading away beyond recognition. Also on the walk, there's a cool painting of BB's guitar, Lucille.

Head up two blocks on 2nd St to **BB King Rd**, which crosses the tracks before running through the black part of town. Street signs along this road make good backdrops for photos.

In early June, the **BB King Hometown Homecoming** (☎ 662-887-4454) welcomes BB to the town with a free outdoor concert at BB King Park on Roosevelt St. At night, a huge crowd heads up the street to Club Ebony (see Eating & Entertainment) in hopes of seeing more of BB.

SLEEPING

INDIANOLA HOTEL & SUITES
☎ 662-887-7477; 601 Hwy 82W; r from $40; P ✂
Along Hwy 82 just after you enter town from the west, this place looks and feels like a chain and maintains comparable standards.

COMFORT INN
☎ 662-887-6611; fax 662-887-1317; 910 Hwy 82E; r $65; P ☂ ✕ ✂
This is a nice-looking outlet of the chain hotel. The pool's a bonus. A convenient stop if you're just breezing through on Hwy 82.

DAYS INN
☎ 601-887-4242; 1015 Hwy 82E; r $45; P
Here's a fairly average example of this decent and inexpensive chain. It's not as nice as Comfort Inn, but the rates are adjusted accordingly.

EATING & ENTERTAINMENT

Indianola isn't known as one of the Delta's better dining hubs, but

BB King
For more than six decades, this man has lived and breathed the blues. BB stands for 'Blues Boy,' which for a time was Riley 'BB' King's nickname. He started out on an Indianola street corner, gained a reputation on Memphis radio and eventually became the king of the blues. He hit No 1 on the R&B charts twice, with 'Three O'Clock Blues' (1951) and 'You Don't Know Me' (1952). In 1970, he crossed over to the pop charts with 'The Thrill is Gone,' which went to No 15. Approaching his 80th birthday, he continues to tour some 250 days a year.

there are a few spots where you can grab a bite. Try **Crown in Town Restaurant** (☎ 662-887-4522; 110 Front Ave; dishes $4-9; ⏰ 9am-5pm Tue-Sat) for catfish and other Mississippi staples.

Indianola's best nightclub is **Club Ebony** (☎ 662-887-9915; 404 Hanna Ave). BB King usually repairs to this snazzy spot after playing his annual Homecoming concert, and there's dancing most weekends and live music occasionally.

Near the tracks, **308 Blues Club & Café** (☎ 662-887-7800; 308 Depot Ave) is a friendly, modern nightclub (founded 2003) that regularly books blues artists on Friday and Saturday nights.

GREENWOOD, MS

Population 18,425

Greenwood is a leafy Delta town with the second-largest cotton market in the US (after Memphis). There's not much blues activity here now, but there certainly was in the past. One of the most disputed events in blues history may have happened here.

On August 16, 1938, Robert Johnson died in the town of Quito, just south of Greenwood, and he is believed to be buried somewhere near here. Johnson seems to have perished in a cloud of smoke – so uncertain are the details of his demise. Debating the spots where Johnson gave his final performance, where he died and where he is buried is an obsessive pastime for many hardcore blues gumshoes. Even if you're not really among that crowd, it would be a shame not to visit at least one of the two graveyards sporting headstones for the legendary blues man.

Greenwood is also one of the best towns in the Delta for dining, making it a good midway stopping point along Hwy 49E between Clarksdale and Vicksburg.

SIGHTS

The **Greenwood Blues Heritage Museum** (☎ 662-451-7800; 222 Howard St; donations accepted; ⏰ 10am-5pm Mon-Sat) is a nice little exhibit that illustrates the role Greenwood played in the development of the Delta blues. Displays highlight musicians with local connections, such as Mississippi John Hurt, Jimmy Reed, BB King, Charlie Patton and Robert Johnson.

Most of the fun in Greenwood comes from chasing the elusive ghost of Robert Johnson. **Johnson St** (the name is coincidental), just south of the railroad tracks, is the main drag in the black part of town. There is no music going on here today, but in the 1930s the best blues men passed through frequently, often to play the sidewalks for change. Robert Johnson was seen here often, as were Sonny Boy Williamson II and Elmore James. Johnson lived his last days a few blocks to the south of the main strip, in the **Baptist Town** neighborhood. Johnson St becomes Carrollton Ave through the heart of this part of town. Some say Robert Johnson was carried

Where Lies Robert Johnson?

Maybe it's pointless to ponder mysteries that will never be solved, but the mythic aura that surrounds Robert Johnson's death has become more tantalizing with time, and the lack of facts just warrants much more than a mere shrug of shoulders.

The most stupefying piece of the Johnson puzzle concerns the whereabouts of his grave. The answer to the question, 'Where Lies Robert Johnson?' is, almost comically, 'Here, there or somewhere else.'

Payne Chapel in Quito was identified by a girlfriend of Johnson's as the place where he was buried, and a simple slab, etched with a guitar and a treble clef, was placed here in 1991. To find it, turn right off Hwy 7 about a quarter-mile south of the bridge onto a narrow, unpaved lane (look for a building marked 'Hardwicke Etter Ginning Systems' opposite the lane). The chapel and graveyard are just up the road.

Johnson's death certificate vaguely cites 'Zion Church' as his final resting place, but this has always been a common name for churches in the Delta. In **Morgan City**, farther down Hwy 7 about 4 miles south of Quito, Johnson has a tombstone in the **Mount Zion MB Church** graveyard. It was put up by Columbia Records in 1991, after the label's phenomenally successful reissue, *The Complete Recordings of Robert Johnson*. This is an impressive obelisk, thoughtfully inscribed on all four sides and adorned by the guitar picks, Mardi Gras beads, CDs and mojos left by the blues man's growing number of fans. To get here from Hwy 7, head east at a sign that says 'Matthew's Wildlife Reserve' and look for the white church a little ways up the road.

There's no headstone for Johnson at the **Little Zion Church** north of Greenwood, but some blues scholars have noted that it's closer to where Johnson reputedly died, tying it more closely to the 'Zion Church' of Johnson's birth certificate. There's little reason to seek out this hard-to-find graveyard, as there's nothing of interest to actually see, but a traveler might ask directions at the **Delta Gallery Blues Museum** (933 Hwy 82W), a grocery store with a modest display of blues photos and curios.

to a house somewhere in Baptist Town after he was poisoned and that he actually died here.

It is widely agreed that Johnson was poisoned during or after a performance at the **Three Forks Store** in nearby **Quito** (reached by taking Hwy 82 west to Hwy 7, and heading south past Itta Bena). But of course there are some who dispute that version of events. The story (related as a firsthand account by David 'Honeyboy' Edwards in his memoir *The World Don't Owe Me Nothing*) is that Johnson had had an affair with the wife of the Three Forks' shopkeeper, who settled the score by slipping a lethal mickey into Johnson's whiskey. Johnson was only 27 years old. Those who consider the poisoning story a tall tale point to a note on Johnson's death certificate speculating that syphilis might have been the cause of death. No autopsy was done, so likely as not the matter will never be settled.

The exact whereabouts of the Three Forks Store are also a matter of some debate. Clarksdale's Delta Blues Museum has a sign from a Three Forks Store that burned down long after Johnson's death, but it is generally believed that this was not the original building, although it may have been the same business after a relocation. A large brown house next to an unnamed bridge on Hwy 7 is reckoned by some to have been the Three Forks Store during the late 1930s (it's a private home now). But then, there were probably other stores bearing the same name.

SLEEPING

BRIDGEWATER INN
☎ 662-453-9265; 501 River Rd; r $75-95; **P** ✕

Greenwood's top choice is this B&B beauty. It's in a 1910 Greek Revival home, with a columned balcony overlooking the Yazoo River. Rooms are filled with antique furnishings and most have private baths with claw-foot tubs. Rates drop significantly if you stay a third night.

RIVERS' INN BED & BREAKFAST
☎ 662-453-5432; riversinn@aol.com; 1109 River Rd; r $58-75; **P** ✕ ✆

Built in 1912, this redbrick home is comfortable, and has a glassed-in garden room where guests are welcome to relax. Rooms are large and tidy, and most have private baths.

BEST INN GREENWOOD
☎ 800-359-4827; 335 Hwy 82W; r $40-47; **P** ✕ ✕

This nondescript motel is convenient and reasonably priced. It offers modem access and free local calls.

EATING & ENTERTAINMENT

SPOONEY'S BBQ
☎ 662-451-7453; 112 E Johnson St; dishes $4-10; ⏰ 11am-7pm Mon-Thu, 11am-1am Fri-Sat

Leroy 'Spooney' Kenter Jr brushes his superb barbecue sauce onto pork ribs, rib tips, chicken, hot links and beef. Before entering his narrow little shop, take a whiff of the meat smokers parked in the adjacent lot. The dive can seat a few people, but most of Spooney's business is done on a take-out basis.

CRYSTAL GRILL
☎ 662-453-6530; 423 Carrollton Ave; dishes $5-17; ⏰ 11am-8pm

A Greenwood landmark since the 1930s, family-owned Crystal Grill has earned a statewide reputation for its 'mile-high' chocolate and coconut meringue pies. Steaks, seafood and fresh vegetables anchor a diverse menu. This is a large place – it seats 200 – and yet it still gets awfully crowded for Sunday dinner. Some locals have been eating here all their lives, and some of the waitresses have been working here for decades.

LUSCO'S
☎ 662-453-5365; 722 Carrollton Ave; dishes $7-20; ☾ 6-9pm Tue-Sat
Another local landmark from the 1930s, Lusco's is often rated among
Mississippi's best restaurants. It qualifies as a set designer's idea of
how a Delta eatery should look: gracefully aged, with tables hidden
in curtained booths. The steaks are broiled to perfection, and the
pompano is to die for. Reservations are a good idea.

MATTIE'S SOUL FOOD
☎ 662-453-5753; 114 W Market St; dishes $4-8; ☾ 7am-2pm Mon-Fri
Here's a sweet spot run by friendly Mattie Smith, who says she
learned to cook from the best – her grandmother. You can fuel up
on a Southern breakfast or fried chicken, catfish, neck bones, yams
and collard greens. The Tuesday specials – meatloaf and chicken and
dumplings – are especially popular.

COTTON ROW CLUB
☎ 662-453-1180; Ramcat Alley; ☾ varies
This is just a little spot of local color. It's a ramshackle social club in
one of Greenwood's oldest buildings, where old men shoot the bull,
play poker and watch football on TV. Sometimes a fisherman will
bring in his day's catch and cook it here for his own eating pleas-
ure, but this is not a restaurant. Anyone is welcome (ah, sure, even
women, who don't exactly frequent the place) to buy a beer from
the Coke machine and sit down just to soak it in. You can even get
your shoes shined here.

BELZONI, MS

Population 2660
Before Belzoni had an official name, it was known far and wide as
'Greasy Row,' and supposedly this was a reference to the many sa-
loons that popped up along this section of the Yazoo River before
there was really a town to speak of here.

By the 1930s, Belzoni was known as a blues magnet. Barrelhouse
pianist Joe Willie 'Pinetop' Perkins was born here in 1913, and Elmore
James spent his teenage years in the town. James, in fact, emulated
Robert Johnson, who frequently passed through Belzoni.

Arthur Big Boy Crudup, whose 'That's Alright Mama' became
Elvis' first hit for Sun, also called Belzoni home. Crudup's rhythmic,
electric blues were an early example of Chicago blues and, some
say, a critical step in the evolution of rock and roll.

Charlie Patton was arrested in Belzoni near the end of his life,
and he sang about the experience in 'High Sheriff Blues,' which he
waxed for posterity in his final recording session.

On the strength of its dozens of catfish farms, surrounding Hum-
phreys County touts itself as the 'catfish capital of the world.' The
World Catfish Festival (☎ 800-408-4838; www.catfishcapitalonline.
com) takes place in Belzoni the first Saturday in April. The one-day
event features live music (usually some fairly white-bread blues)

and culminates with a fish fry ($7) and the crowning of Miss Catfish (who, regrettably, does not show up wearing a scaly fish suit). Belzoni also celebrates its catfish-producing renown with colorful catfish statues all over town.

On the same day as the Catfish Festival, Belzoni also has its annual **African American Heritage Buffalo Fish Festival** (☎ 662-247-1471; www.buffalofishfestival.com), a smaller, all-day affair that features some quality blues, soul and jazz performances. The buffalo fish is an edible humpbacked sucker found up and down the Mississippi River valley. Significantly, this festival has recently been staged as a protest against the catfish industry, which employs many black laborers but few black executives.

Kozy Korner Cafe (☎ 662-247-9942; 109 S Railway Ave) is Belzoni's biggest and best juke joint, with friendly folks and a good jukebox. It's a good spot for shooting some pool and knocking back a few cold ones with the locals.

Belzoni is about 20 miles south of Indianola via Hwy 49W and about 30 miles south of Greenwood via Hwy 7.

ON THE ROAD

South of Belzoni, the Yazoo River wends its way to its namesake Yazoo City, and Hwy 49W follows a different route to the same spot. But first it's worth taking a slight detour along Hwy 14 back to Hwy 61 and the town of **Rolling Fork**, to see where McKinley Morganfield, aka Muddy Waters, was born in 1914. The town has a **Muddy Waters monument** on its courthouse square.

Mississippi John Hurt

The town of **Avalon**, on Hwy 7, 11 miles north of Greenwood, is where Mississippi John Hurt (1892–1966) was born and lived his entire life. A man of small stature and a bright, worldly-wise demeanor, Hurt had an easy, homespun way with words and his guitar-picking was uncommonly sweet and lyrical. He recorded a few sides in the late 1920s that stood apart from records by other, more hard-edged Delta players, and he then simply returned to tilling the fields for three decades.

Hurt was rediscovered during the folk revival in the 1960s and enjoyed a few years of well-earned recognition. He performed at the Newport Folk Festival, in New York coffeehouses and even on the *Tonight Show*. He recorded three beautiful albums for Vanguard in 1966 and died in November of that year.

He is buried in Avalon, in a grove of trees at the end of a country road. It can be confusing to find it but well worth the trouble to pay your respects. Follow Hwy 7 north of Greenwood, head east on Hwy 41 for nearly 4 miles (past the pavement's end) and turn left up a rutted road and through some woods, about 1 mile, to the cemetery, marked by orange ribbons tied round the trees. Hurt's simple tombstone is marked: 'John S Hurt.'

From Rolling Fork, Hwy 16 heads east back to Hwy 49W, passing through the Delta National Forest and Holly Bluff en route.

The name **Yazoo City** is familiar today thanks mostly to the Yazoo record label, which has released so many early Delta blues recordings in tastefully packaged CD compilations (many featuring brilliant R Crumb illustrations on the covers). Tommy McClennan was born and raised in Yazoo, but there's no blues action here these days. The town is pretty, and it has far more than its share of good barbecue and soul food eateries.

Hines Broadlake Grocery (☎ 662-746-6518; 45 Shaffer Rd at Hwy 49; dishes $2-9; ✆ 6am-6pm Mon-Sat) is a great little roadhouse that does catfish, barbecue and hot links. **Stub's** (☎ 662-746-1204; 1902 Jerry Clower Blvd; dishes $6-12; ✆ 11am-9pm Mon-Fri, 11am-2pm Sun) is a simple, utilitarian place that'll just knock you out with hickory-smoked ribs, pork and chicken. It's cafeteria style at lunchtime, with a full menu at night.

Riverbend Catfish House (☎ 662-746-6081; 1017 S Industrial Pky; dishes $5-14; ✆ 11am-9pm Tue-Thu, 11am-10pm Fri-Sat) will set you up with plates of catfish, steak and sandwiches. **JJ's Krispy Krunchy Chicken** (☎ 662-746-1099; 220 Martin Luther King Dr; dishes $2-6; ✆ 11am-6:30pm Mon-Sat) is a down-home fried chicken take-out stand.

East of Yazoo City, Hwy 49 beelines to Jackson, passing **Bentonia** along the way. Fans of Nehemia 'Skip' James will have heard of this town. James and his contemporary Jack Owens hailed from Bentonia, and both combined eerie falsetto vocals and cross-note guitar tuning, otherwise known as 'Spanish' tuning. Their distinctive style came to be known as the Bentonia school of Delta blues. The style was tagged 'devil blues' by those who were understandably spooked by it. James' recording 'Devil Got My Woman' captures Bentonia blues at its best, and Owens' 'Must Have Been the Devil' is very similar.

Medgar Evers

Jackson was home to Medgar Evers, the NAACP field secretary who was murdered in 1963, at the height of the civil rights struggle. Evers had led boycotts of segregationist businesses, and he was investigating the Citizens' Council, a segregationist band suspected of coordinating repressive acts against blacks throughout Mississippi.

Shortly after midnight on June 12, 1963, Evers was shot in the driveway of his home in a northwest neighborhood in the city. He died within the hour.

His accused assailant, Byron de la Beckwith, was an ardent segregationist from Greenwood. Two trials ended in a deadlocked jury, but after new evidence was uncovered Beckwith was finally convicted of Evers' murder in 1994, 31 years later.

Evers' home (☎ 601-977-7839; 2332 Margaret Walker Alexander Dr) remains a private residence, but tours can be arranged by appointment.

James recorded some highly collectible 78rpm sides in the late 1920s and early '30s, then turned his back on the blues in favor of the spiritual life. He returned to immense popular demand in the 1960s, playing before mostly white audiences although he was clearly embittered by racial issues in America. Owens was the lesser known of the two and did not record until he was an old man, but he lived until 1997, nearly three decades after James' death, so he enjoyed the spotlight as Bentonia's finest for a long time.

Bentonia's **Blue Front Cafe** (☎ 662-755-2278; 107 E Railroad Ave) is one of the absolute coolest juke joints still standing in the Delta. It's just a humble white structure on a rural road, and live blues are played on some Sunday nights.

JACKSON, MS

Population 395,000

Mississippi's capital city is outside the Delta, but not by much. Farish St, the axis of the black side of downtown, was a regular stop for traveling blues men, and many artists recorded here. Tommy Johnson, Skip James, Otis Spann, Sonny Boy Williamson II and Elmore James all lived in Jackson for a spell. Jackson was also a focal point during the civil rights struggle. The historic downtown has a ghost-town feel today, even though it's where the state government operates. There are still a few blues clubs in the area and some great old restaurants.

SIGHTS

In its early-20th-century heyday, **Farish St**, north of Capitol St, was the hub of black political, economic, social, religious and cultural life in the state. The district has badly deteriorated, but some blues landmarks remain standing along the 200 and 300 blocks, including **Speir's Music Store** (225 Farish St), which is marked by a faded sign for a more recent furniture business. HC Speir ran his music store here during the 1920s and sold records and guitars to a predominantly black clientele. To accelerate record sales, Speir sought out new talent in the Delta and arranged recording sessions with record labels dealing in 'race' music. Charlie Patton, Tommy Johnson, Skip James and Robert Johnson were among the artists who might never have recorded had it not been for Speir.

Two record labels set up small studios on Farish St during the 1950s, and their buildings still stand. These were Johnny Vincent's **Ace Records** (241 Farish St), where Earl King recorded, and **Trumpet Records** (309 Farish St), where Sonny Boy Williamson II and Elmore James recorded.

The **Alamo Theater** (☎ 601-352-3365; 333 Farish St) is a restored landmark from the 1950s where legendary talent shows and live music are frequently staged.

SLEEPING

Jackson has numerous chains along I-55 north and south of downtown.

SUN-N-SAND MOTEL
☎ 601-354-2501; 401 N Lamar St; r $40; P ⊠ ⧑

Right downtown, this orange and turquoise relic from the early '60s is the swinging place to stay in Jackson. Polynesian decor and a trapezoidal swimming pool compensate for the lack of an actual beach, but they are mere window dressing for the time-warp lounge with its vinyl barstools and decidedly unhip local clientele.

POINDEXTER PARK INN
☎ 601-944-1392; 803 Deer Park St; r $59; P ⊠ ⊠

The grand old home of Mississippi's second governor is now a lovely B&B. The old neighborhood has declined a bit since George Poindexter's time, but guests will be comfortable amid the antiques and claw-foot tubs of his former house. Owner Marcia Weaver will gladly point the way to live blues. The inn is a bit north of downtown, just east of I-55.

EATING & ENTERTAINMENT

MAYFLOWER CAFE
☎ 601-355-4122; 123 W Capitol St; dishes $6-18; ⓒ 11am-10pm Mon-Sat

A giant flashing neon sign beckons diners into this sweet old spot, owned by cigar-chomping Mr Mike. It's an authentic greasy spoon, with worn counter and stools, where the hash has been slung since 1935. The blue-plate lunches ($6) smothered in gravy are excellent.

PEACHES RESTAURANT
☎ 601-354-9267; 327 N Farish St; dishes $4-12; ⓒ 6am-9pm Mon-Sat

On Farish St, this great soul food spot (here since 1961) exerts a natural pull on blues fans, with its smothered chicken, collard and turnip greens, butter beans, pig ears, chitlins and the like. You can also order a greasy breakfast here. There's a good jukebox. No credit cards.

E&L'S BAR-B-Q
☎ 601-355-5035; 1111 Bailey Ave; dishes $4-10

Barbecue lovers swear by this smoky dive, where ribs, rib tips and links make the stomach growl in anticipation. You can also order pan trout here.

HAL & MAL'S
☎ 601-948-0888; 200 S Commerce St; dishes $7-18; ⓒ 11am-2am Mon-Sat

Live blues, jazz and R&B bands often play this popular brewpub, where the menu features New Orleans fare, such as red beans and rice, po-boy sandwiches, burgers and seafood. The meat-and-three lunches are another big draw. It's near the Old Capitol, above the Pascagoula St underpass.

930 BLUES CAFE
☎ 601-948-3344; 930 N Congress St
In an old house a couple of blocks north of the Capitol, the 930 Blues Cafe features live blues most nights, even during the early evening happy hour. National acts pass through on the weekends, and house bands keep things rocking the rest of the time. The club draws a mixed crowd.

FIELDS
☎ 601-353-1400; cnr Farish & Griffith Sts
This juke, on the historic strip, is ordinarily a quiet watering hole for locals, but it has a blues jam on Monday night.

VICKSBURG, MS

Population 27,500
Vicksburg is generally considered the southern edge of the vaguely defined Mississippi Delta and as such played a peripheral role in the development of the blues. However, this is where songwriter Willie Dixon came from. After joining Chess Records in Chicago, Dixon provided Muddy Waters and Howlin' Wolf with some of their biggest hits, such as 'I'm Your Hootchie Coohie Man,' 'Back Door Man,' 'Spoonful' and 'The Little Red Rooster.' Little Brother Montgomery was also from Vicksburg.

Long before the blues came about, Vicksburg gained notoriety as a strategic focal point in the Civil War, thanks to its location on a high bluff on the Mississippi River. Union General Ulysses S Grant besieged the city for 47 days until its surrender on July 4, 1863, at which point the North gained the dominant hand over North America's greatest river.

The major sights are readily accessible from I-20 exit 4B (Clay St). Get information at the **visitors center** (☎ 601-636-9421, 800-221-3536; cnr Clay & Washington Sts). The cobblestone blocks of Washington St, near the River, are lined with restaurants and shops. Riverboat casinos glitter down on the banks.

SIGHTS

MARGARET'S GROCERY
☎ 601-638-1163; 4535 N Washington St; ⏱ varies
As you drive down Hwy 61 from the north into Vicksburg, you can't help but notice the huge red, yellow, white and pink towers that engulf this old grocery store. By all means, pull off and inspect this more closely. It has been Rev HD Dennis' obsession to turn the grocery 'into a palace,' as he promised his wife, Margaret, he would do when she married him two decades ago. The Reverend has added

a chapel fashioned from an old school bus, and throughout the compound he's scrawled verses from the Bible. Clearly this ongoing work of art is no idle hobby. The store itself is no longer open, but you can often find Rev Dennis on hand, touching up the paint or adding a few new bricks. He's a warm, talkative octogenarian who enjoys chatting about the Bible.

OLD COURT HOUSE MUSEUM

☎ 601-636-0741; www.oldcourthouse.org; 1008 Cherry St; admission $3; 8:30am-4:30pm Mon-Sat, 1:30-4:30pm Sun

Vicksburg's most important landmark was designed and built in 1858 by skilled slaves. The cost of construction: a mere $10,000. John Jackson was the architect. The exhibits inside the building relate Vicksburg history in colorful, sometimes overly rosy terms, particularly where the subject of slavery is covered. Amid shocking Klan hoods and old yellow newspapers, there are some genuinely lighthearted curiosities, such as an exhibit on the 'Minnié Ball Pregnancy,' which maintains that in a battle at Raymond, Mississippi, a shot was fired through a soldier's reproductive organs and continued on into the reproductive organs of a female observer. Naturally, the ball successfully impregnated the woman.

NATIONAL MILITARY PARK & CEMETERY

☎ 601-636-0583; www.nps.gov/vick; per car $5; 8am-5pm

North of I-20 on Clay St, this Civil War site is the city's main attraction. The park preserves 1858 acres where the Union army laid siege to Vicksburg. An 18-mile driving tour through the rolling wooded hills leads to historic markers explaining key events that occurred here. The cemetery, in which nearly 17,000 Union soldiers are buried, is in the northern end of the park. A museum relates some fascinating, oft-overlooked history.

SLEEPING

BATTLEFIELD INN

☎ 601-638-5811, 800-359-9363; www.battlefieldinn.org; 4137 I-20 Frontage Rd; r $45-80; P ☒ ☒

It looks like your average roadside motel, but Battlefield Inn pampers its visitors with free cocktails and snacks in the early evening and a free buffet breakfast in the morning. Rooms are tidy and comfortable. It's very close to the National Military Park.

CEDAR GROVE

☎ 601-636-1000, 800-862-1300; www.cedargroveinn.com; r $115-225; P ☒ ☒

Vicksburg's showpiece B&B is this 1840 Greek Revival mansion surrounded by 4 acres of landscaped gardens overlooking the river. A Union cannonball remains lodged in a parlor wall, and the house retains many original antiques and gaslit chandeliers. All that's missing is Scarlett and Rhett. All rooms have private baths.

THE CORNERS
☎ 601-636-7421, 800-444-7421; www.thecorners.com; 601 Klein St; r $90-130; P X ⌘

This B&B is in an elegant 1873 home atop a bluff overlooking the valley. Guest rooms are decked out with canopy beds, and some have fireplaces, private porches and views. The back gallery is a fine spot to claim a rocking chair and enjoy a refreshing lemonade. All rooms have private baths. Kids and pets are welcome.

HILLCREST MOTEL
☎ 601-638-1491, 40 Hwy 80; r $32; P ⌘

At the bottom of the price range, this perfectly serviceable motel has unbeatable rates.

EATING

WALNUT HILLS
☎ 601-638-4910; 1214 Adams St; dishes $7-12; ⌚ 11am-9pm Mon-Fri, 11am-2pm Sun

Your best bet in Vicksburg is this charming old house near downtown, which serves traditional Southern favorites. Daily menus include old faves like fried chicken and country-fried steak, Southern cooked vegetables, biscuits and cornbread. Meals are served family-style at big round tables (you can also just order your own 'blue plate special').

GOLDIE'S TRAIL BBQ
☎ 601-636-9839; 4127 S Washington St; dishes $4-11; ⌚ noon-9pm Mon-Sat; noon-8pm Sun

Vicksburg's best barbecue is served at this family-friendly restaurant offering pork, beef or chicken. The meat here is not as good as we've come to expect from the Delta, but will do the trick if you really need some BBQ in Vicksburg.

ROWDY'S FAMILY CATFISH SHACK
☎ 601-638-2375; 60 Hwy 27; dishes $4-14; ⌚ 11am-9pm Sun-Thu

Mississippi pond-raised catfish is sliced thin, battered, fried and served up with hush puppies, skillet cornbread and French fries in this old standby near I-20. You can also get burgers and hearty sandwiches.

ENTERTAINMENT

Vicksburg's live-music scene is dominated by the riverside casinos. **Bottleneck Blues Bar** (☎ 601-638-1000), in the Ameristar Casino, is a modern facility modeled on a 1930 theater. Blues are often on the bill here; national acts and regional artists pass through on a regular basis. **Hwy 61 South** (☎ 601-636-7575), in the Rainbow Casino, generally offers less prominent blues talents.

ON THE ROAD

At **Port Gibson**, about midway between Vicksburg and Natchez, Hwy 61 intersects with the Natchez Trace Parkway. From here, it's possible to take the Trace for a spell down to Natchez, or you can detour northward on the Trace to Jackson, if you haven't already been to the capital city.

Port Gibson has a fine pit stop in **Grant's Place** (☎ 601-437-0079; 1091 Old Hwy 61N; dishes $4-7). Get you some fried chicken and mashed potatoes smothered in gravy with turnip greens and cornbread on the side.

NATCHEZ, MS

Population 20,000; Map 5

This is the opulent side of the Old South, where white fluted pillars appear to converge somewhere above the tops of ancient live oak trees. The wedding-cake antebellum architecture of Natchez, perched on a bluff overlooking the Mississippi, attracts many tourists, especially during the spring and fall when local mansions are opened to visitors.

Natchez had one of the busiest slave markets in the South, and thousands of slaves worked on the local plantations, creating one of the wealthiest pre-war towns in the country. The town remains sharply segregated to this day.

In 1940, the Natchez Rhythm Club, the most popular black nightclub in town, burned to the ground, killing 260 patrons and musicians. The tragedy resounded throughout the state, and Howlin' Wolf honored the victims in the song 'Natchez Burning.'

Drop by the **visitors center** (☎ 601-446-6345, 800-647-6724; www.natchez.ms.us; 640 S Canal St; 🕑 8:30am-5pm Mon-Sat, 9am-4pm Sun) to find out which houses are open for tours.

SIGHTS

Many of Natchez's historic houses are open for tours year-round. Only Melrose has re-created slave quarters as a reminder of the unpleasant reality behind the area's affluence.

MELROSE
☎ 601-446-5790; 1 Melrose-Montebello Parkway; admission $6; 🕑 9am-4pm
Run by the National Park Service, Melrose is a grand plantation estate. The slave quarters have exhibits on the history of slavery.

HOUSE ON ELLICOTT'S HILL
☎ 601-442-2011; 211 N Canal St; admission $6; 🕑 9am-4pm
The oldest property open for tours is on a hill where Andrew Ellicott raised the American flag in 1798 in defiance of the Spanish rule.

LONGWOOD
☎ 601-442-5193; 140 Lower Woodville Rd; admission $6; ⏱ 9am-4:30pm
Intriguingly, construction of this grand octagonal house began in 1860, but was disrupted by the Civil War and never completed. From downtown Natchez, Homochitto St heads southeast past Hwy 84, where it becomes Lower Woodville Rd.

STANTON HALL
☎ 601-442-6282; 401 High St; admission $6; ⏱ 9am-4:30pm
This palatial 1857 mansion, a gleaming white neoclassical structure amid striking live oaks, has a good lunch spot.

MUSEUM OF AFRICAN-AMERICAN HISTORY & CULTURE
☎ 601-445-0728; 301 Main St; donations requested; ⏱ 1-5pm Wed-Sat
This museum recounts local black history from the 1880s to the 1950s in a personal way with period kitchens, costumes and accounts of the Natchez Rhythm Club fire.

FORK OF THE ROAD
There's not much to see here, but this junction of St Catherine St, D'Evereux St and the regrettably named Liberty Rd was the site of the town's slave market. Most slaves sold here were marched from the Atlantic states to Natchez and then sold to cotton-growing landholders in the Deep South.

SLEEPING

MONMOUTH
☎ 601-442-5852, 800-828-4531; www.monmouthplantation.com; 36 Melrose Ave; r $165-220; Ⓟ ✕ ⌘
A luxurious setting for a nervous breakdown – full-blown Southern splendor is what we're talking about here, but with key modern comforts thrown in. Rooms are outfitted with Posture-Pedic beds, fireplaces and private baths, and the extensive, atmospheric grounds include moss-draped oaks, a croquet court, fishing ponds, a wooded hiking trail and tennis courts. Leave your mojo in the car glove box.

NATCHEZ GUEST HOUSE
☎ 601-442-8848, 866-442-8848; www.natchezguesthouse.com; 201 N Pearl St; r $80-200; Ⓟ ✕ ⌘
In the heart of town, this historic inn, built in 1840, doesn't have the acreage of some of Natchez's finest houses but is certainly posh enough. Rooms have four-poster beds, and the lush courtyard restaurant hosts a Sunday blues brunch.

NATCHEZ STATE PARK
☎ 601-442-2658; campsites $9, cabins $62
This shady, 50-site campground is 10 miles north of town at the

start of the Natchez Trace. The pre-fab air-conditioned cabins sleep up to six people.

NATCHEZ INN
☎ 601-442-0221; 218 John R Junkin Dr; r $35; P ✕
This no-frills budget choice offers basic but clean rooms.

EATING & ENTERTAINMENT

CARRIAGE HOUSE
☎ 601-445-5151; 401 High St; dishes $8-12; ☀ 11am-2:30pm
A plate of expertly fried chicken on the grounds of Stanton Hall will surely enhance your Natchez day. This is a good spot to try those fried green tomatoes you've heard about.

MAMMY'S CUPBOARD
☎ 601-445-8957; 555 Hwy 61S; dishes $3-8; ☀ 11am-2pm Tue-Sat
Strangely enough, this place offers an opportunity to peek beneath the skirt of an old racist icon. It's a real head-turner, built in 1940 to look like a 28-foot tall black mammy, with her billowing skirts enclosing a small lunch room. (Although, strangely, a recent paint job appears to have turned her into a *white* mammy.) It ain't exactly cute, but it is certainly of historic interest, and confronting this trace of minstrelsy is just the honest thing to do. Daily specials include chicken pot pie and red beans and rice, plus homemade desserts.

FAT MAMA'S TAMALES
☎ 601-442-4548; 500 S Canal St; tamales $6/dozen; ☀ 11am-9pm Mon & Thu, 11am-10pm Fri-Sat, noon-7pm Sun
It's touristy, yes, but this little log cabin is a fun spot. The tamales are the main event, and the 'knock you naked' margaritas are the perfect supporting cast. Or is it the other way around?

COCK OF THE WALK
☎ 601-446-8920; 200 N Broadway; dishes $8-15; ☀ 5-10pm
With silly waiters strutting about like 19th-century river men – turkey feathers in wide-brim hats and the whole bit – dining at this bluff establishment is no authentic experience. But you'll enjoy the cornbread, flipped from a skillet at your table, and the catfish dinner.

BISCUITS & BLUES
☎ 601-446-9922; 315 Main St; ☀ noon-10pm
You can eat OK ribs and wings here, or just get a beer and enjoy the live blues on weekends.

ON THE ROAD

Hwy 61 continues into **Louisiana**. If you don't have hotel reservations for New Orleans, drop by the **State Welcome Center** here to see if they can offer discount rooms. You can often get unbelievable deals in three-star French Quarter hotels.

Louisiana's state capital is **Baton Rouge**, about 75 miles north of New Orleans. The town comes alive the last week of April for the **Baton Rouge Blues Week** (www.louisianamusic.com). This event coincides with the New Orleans Jazz Festival, so if you're heading to the Big Easy for that, it might be worth checking the Blues Week program to see if a stop in Baton Rouge is worthwhile. The local blues scene is headed by Tabby Thomas and Henry Gray. Chris Thomas King, one of the best contemporary blues pickers, is Tabby's son.

Duck into **Poor Boy Lloyd's** (☎ 225-387-2271; 205 Florida St; dishes $3-10; ☽ 7am-3pm Mon-Fri) for chicken and dumplings or an oyster po-boy. **Tabby's Blues Box and Heritage Hall** (☎ 225-387-9715; 244 Lafayette) is where Tabby Thomas' house band holds court on a regular basis.

NEW ORLEANS, LA

Population 500,000; Map 6

New Orleans is rightfully thought of as a jazz city, not a blues hot spot, for it was here that most of the early innovations of jazz took place. New Orleans is commonly referred to as the 'birthplace' of jazz, which implies that the music started here. It is also sometimes called the 'cradle of jazz,' which more accurately suggests that the music was rocked and burped here after having sprouted up in various parts of the US. But the development of jazz coincided with the emergence of the blues, and early New Orleans trumpet players and piano players were, in fact, often playing variations on the blues. New Orleans did have its share of midcentury blues men, too, including Guitar Slim, Earl King and Snooks Eaglin.

And so, with no apology, the blues and barbecue tour ends up in the hometown of Buddy Bolden, Jelly Roll Morton, King Oliver, Louis Armstrong, Mahalia Jackson, Professor Longhair, Irma Thomas and an endless retinue of songsters who have sprouted from New Orleans' fertile musical soil.

New Orleans is also a fun and beautiful city, filled with bars and jazz clubs and restaurants, and its festivals are among the most exciting in the country. **Mardi Gras** (mid-February or early March) is legendary and, for some, overwhelming. The **French Quarter Festival** (mid-April) is a 'warm-up' to Jazz Fest, with great music and delicious food. **New Orleans Jazz & Heritage Festival** (www.nojazzfest.com; late April and early May), held over two consecutive weekends, is simply one of the best music festivals in the US, with jazz, R&B, gospel, country and world music stages.

New Orleans is a fascinating place, worthy of several days' visit. This book focuses on the considerable musical attractions of the city. If you're intention is to explore New Orleans more thoroughly, Lonely Planet's *New Orleans* city guide will serve you well.

SIGHTS

NEW ORLEANS JAZZ EXHIBIT

☎ 504-568-6968; 400 Esplanade Ave; admission $5; ⊙ 9am-5pm Tue-Sun

Taking up an entire floor of the Old US Mint, this exhibit has an intriguing assemblage of memorabilia and photographs, as well as dented horns, busted snare drums and homemade gut-stringed bass fiddles played by some of New Orleans' cherished musicians. Admission also gets you into the Houma Indian Arts Museum, in the same building, with displays of impressive and humorous contemporary Native American art.

HOGAN JAZZ ARCHIVES

☎ 504-865-5688; Joseph Merrick Jones Hall, 3rd floor, 304 Freret St; admission free; ⊙ 8:30am-5pm Mon-Fri, 9:30am-1pm Sat

This specialized research library, uptown on the Tulane University campus, is worth going to if you're seriously into jazz history. Most of its great wealth of material is not on exhibit, but the librarian will retrieve items from the stacks for you. The collection includes rare

78rpm records that you can listen to. Curator Bruce Raeburn is a good man to talk to about the music, and the Storyville Room, with its emphasis on Jelly Roll Morton, is worth a gander.

LOUIS ARMSTRONG PARK

A public space bearing Satchmo's name in this particular spot, on Rampart St just outside the French Quarter, makes perfect sense, because during the mid-19th century, **Congo Square** was here. Slaves and free persons of color congregated at the market just outside the city walls that once lined Rampart St. Significantly, African dances and percussion were permitted here. This was a rare phenomenon, as African culture was strictly repressed in slave quarters throughout the South. The entertainment at Congo Square helped keep local musicians in touch with African polyrhythms, which would be a key ingredient in jazz.

Statues of Louis Armstrong and Sidney Bechet commemorate two of New Orleans' greatest jazz soloists. Events take place in the park during Jazz Fest. During quiet times, some consider it unsafe to wander alone in the park.

ST LOUIS CEMETERY NO 1
admission free; ⌣ 8am-3pm

New Orleans' oldest cemetery dates to 1789 and is uncommonly beautiful in its state of gradual decay. Wandering through the statuary and ornate ironwork, you'll encounter the tombs of some interesting New Orleans characters. Voodoo Queen Marie Laveau purportedly rests here. Homer Plessy, famed for losing the landmark Supreme Court decision that ushered in the Jim Crow years, is here, along with the city's first black mayor, Ernest 'Dutch' Morial. Be careful not to venture into the cemetery alone; it's best to coincide your visit with a tour, to ensure your safety. The cemetery is on Basin St, near Louis Armstrong Park.

J&M MUSIC SHOP
☎ 504-522-1336; 840 N Rampart St; ⌣ 10am-9pm

Cossimo Matassa's studio, where some of New Orleans' biggest R&B records were made, closed down years ago. The site is still standing, though, and is now home to Hula Mae's Laundry. The snazzy old J&M sign remains embedded in the threshold, and inside there's a little exhibit by the dryers and folding tables. This historic spot is where Fats Domino and Dave Bartholomew established the 'New Orleans sound' and Lloyd Price waxed 'Lawdy Miss Clawdy' in the early 1950s.

BACKSTREET MUSEUM
☎ 504-522-4806; 1116 St Claude Ave; donations accepted; ⌣ 10am-5pm Tue-Sat

The former Blandin's Funeral Home has been converted into this charming 'powerhouse of knowledge.' The subject matter here is the venerated traditions of black New Orleans, with a particular emphasis on jazz funerals and the Mardi Gras Indians. There are some stunning Indian suits on display here. Request a guided tour.

SLEEPING

GENTRY HOUSE

☎ 504-525-4433; www.gentryhouse.com; 1031 St Ann St; r $85-125; 🔀

A converted double-shotgun with a peaceful courtyard, Sadie Gentry's homey guesthouse is half a block from Rampart St jazz clubs. Furnishings are well used but quite comfortable, and rooms have small kitchens. Credit cards are not accepted.

LAMOTHE HOUSE

☎ 504-947-1161, 800-367-5858; www.new-orleans.org; 621 Esplanade Ave; r $59-134; P 🔀 🔀

This grand old inn is a prime jumping-off point for prowling the nightlife of the lower Quarter and Frenchmen St in the Faubourg Marigny. Rooms are furnished with the sorts of antiques you won't feel guilty stumbling into after a healthy night out.

PRYTANIA PARK HOTEL

☎ 504-524-0427, 800-862-1984; www.prytaniaparkhotel.com; 1525 Prytania St; r from $59

On St Charles Ave in the Lower Garden District, this is a restored 1850s guesthouse with a large modern addition. Rooms are small but nicely appointed with refrigerators and microwaves. Streetcars to the Quarter are just a block away.

JOSEPHINE GUEST HOUSE

☎ 504-524-6361, 800-779-6361; 1450 Josephine St; r $115-165; 🔀

This Lower Garden District house has many loyal repeat visitors who enjoy the hospitable environment. There are just six rooms, and it's only one block to the St Charles streetcars.

COLUMNS HOTEL

☎ 504-899-9308, 800-445-9308; www.thecolumns.com; 3811 St Charles Ave; r $110-180; 🔀

Built in 1883, the Columns is one of the grand establishments along leafy St Charles Ave. The glory doesn't stop at the magnificent porch columns: the downstairs bar is one of the city's most festive, and a mahogany staircase leads up to unfussy, nicely priced rooms.

BENACHI HOUSE

☎ 504-525-7040, 800-308-7040; www.nolabb.com; 2257 Bayou Rd; r $89-135; P 🔀

Half a block from Esplanade Ave and near the Fairgrounds (where Jazz Fest takes place) is this spectacular 1859 Greek Revival mansion amid spacious gardens. The four guestrooms are handsome indeed, with original details and mahogany furnishings. Only one has a private bath, however. This is traditional Southern style at a reasonable price.

MAZANT GUEST HOUSE

☎ 504-944-2662; 906 Mazant St; r shared/private bath $40/44; P 🔀 🔀

Music lovers seem to know about this spot in the Bywater. It's an attractive, two-story farmhouse with a common kitchen and 11 varied rooms. Furnishings are slightly faded but comfortable, and Vaughan's bar is just a few blocks away. Credit cards are not accepted.

EATING

CAFÉ DU MONDE
☎ 504-581-2914; 800 Decatur St; beignets $2.50; ☽ 24hr

This New Orleans institution opposite Jackson Square is a great place to have a café au lait and piping-hot *beignets* (deep-fried pastries dusted with powdered sugar).

UGLESICH'S
☎ 504-523-8751; 1238 Baronne St; lunch $8-15; ☽ 11am-2pm Mon-Fri

It's a trek to get to this little family-run joint, but no one's ever left saying it wasn't worth the trouble. Uglesich's dishes up authentic Louisiana cuisine in suitable down-home environs. Sample from the top-notch oyster bar before feasting on fresh seafood specials. The 'trout muddy waters' ($13) qualifies as a local classic. Or you can settle for a drop-dead-delicious po-boy sandwich.

NAPOLEON HOUSE
☎ 504-524-9752; 500 Chartres St; ☽ 11am-5pm Mon, 11am-midnight Tue-Fri, 11am-7pm Sun

This ancient haunt (opened in 1797) has seen it all, including years of decay. Its well-worn stuccoed walls haven't seen a dab of paint in what must be decades, lending the place an above-it-all sort of dignity. Grab a muffuletta and a beer here in this atmospheric landmark.

DOOKY CHASE RESTAURANT
☎ 504-821-0600; 2301 Orleans Ave; dishes $6-25; ☽ 11:30am-10pm Sun-Thu, 11:30am-midnight Fri-Sat

Long ago, Dooky's was the stomping grounds of civil rights leaders and legendary jazz musicians. The interior is somewhat staid and formal, but Dooky's bar, entered via a side entrance, has a much more down-home environment and serves fried chicken and gumbo. It's in a dodgy part of town, so be sure to park in the restaurant's private lot.

CENTRAL GROCERY
☎ 504-523-1620; 923 Decatur St; sandwiches $6-8; ☽ 8am-5:30pm Mon-Sat, 9am-5:30pm Sun

The muffuletta sandwich was invented by a Sicilian immigrant here way back in 1906. Today, it's still the best place in town to get the sandwich, a round, seeded loaf of bread filled with ham, salami and provolone and drizzled with oily olive relish. Buy one to share.

PARASOL'S
☎ 504-899-2054; 2533 Constance St; po-boys $6; ☽ 11am-10pm

Locals will almost always direct you to this Irish Channel bar for the finest shredded roast beef po-boys.

DOMILISE'S PO-BOYS
☎ 504-899-9126; 5240 Annunciation St; po-boys $7; ☯ 11am-7pm Mon-Sat

If you're looking for a humble little shack with a great big fryer, look no further. The fried shrimp po-boy qualifies as essential Uptown eating.

BYWATER BBQ
☎ 504-944-4445; 3162 Dauphine St; dishes $6-14; ☯ 6am-10pm Mon-Fri, 11am-10pm Sat-Sun

New Orleans isn't known for its barbecue, but you'll find the good stuff here, where spare ribs, chicken and pulled pork are served in heaping quantities. Grab a patio table in back.

ELIZABETH'S
☎ 504-944-9272; 601 Gallier St; dishes $3-8; ☯ 7am-2:30pm Tue-Sat

This spotless little eatery in the Bywater offers the best deals in town for breakfast and lunch. Everything on the menu exceeds expectations in quality and quantity, including heaps of grits, omelettes, po-boys, pancakes, fresh biscuits and brilliant daily specials.

ENTERTAINMENT

MID-CITY ROCK & BOWL
☎ 504-482-3133l 4133 S Carrollton Ave; cover $5-10

Get thee to the Rock & Bowl to see some of New Orleans' best R&B, blues and zydeco music. You can also bowl a few frames between sets. It's at the corner of Tulane and Carrollton.

DONNA'S BAR & GRILL
☎ 504-596-6914; 800 N Rampart St; cover $5-15

This little sweatbox touts itself as New Orleans' 'brass band headquarters.' Local jazz talent gets booked, and those who aren't often stop by to jam. Mondays the club dishes out free red beans and barbecue.

VAUGHAN'S
☎ 504-947-5562; 800 Lesseps St; cover $10

Swing down to the lower Bywater on Thursday night for Kermit Ruffins' weekly jazz jam at Vaughan's. The consummate showman, Kermit makes the deal more enticing by serving up barbecue from the back of his pickup truck. Show starts around 11pm.

SPOTTED CAT
☎ 504-943-3887; 623 Frenchmen St

The friendly patrons don't seem to mind sharing a good thing in this little local spot, known for its smart jazz and swing combos and stylishly casual ambience. Admission's free, but the beer's marked up.

HOUSE OF BLUES
☎ 504-529-2583; 255 Decatur St; cover $7-25

One of the best live-music venues in town books fine rock, country and alternative acts. The Sunday gospel brunch will fortify your soul.

TIPITINA'S
☎ 504-895-8477; 501 Napoleon Ave; cover $10-20

Tip's is New Orleans' legendary music club. On the street, look for the bust of Henry Roland Byrd (1918–80), or 'Professor Longhair,' whose 1953 hit 'Tipitina' inspired the club's name.

PRESERVATION HALL
☎ 504-522-2841; 726 St Peter St; cover $5

A historically significant place, this worn music hall attracts veteran jazz musicians. Get there early to get a seat, or stand outside and listen through the open shutters.

FUNKY BUTT ON CONGO SQUARE
☎ 504-558-0872; 714 N Rampart St; cover $5-15

With a sexy Jazz Age atmosphere, the Funky Butt turns up the heat with modern jazz, Latin rhythms and a lively crowd.

MAPLE LEAF BAR
☎ 504-866-9359; 8316 Oak St; cover $5-10

By the Riverbend, Maple Leaf packs a wild crowd into its pressed-tin music hall. Look for blues man Walter 'Wolfman' Washington, zydeco star Rockin' Dopsie Jr and the Rebirth Jazz Band.

SNUG HARBOR
☎ 504-949-0696; 626 Frenchmen St; cover $10-25

This club in Faubourg Marigny is the city's premier contemporary jazz venue. Expect regular performances by Ellis Marsalis (Wynton and Branford's dad) and a revolving door of touring artists.

ERNIE K-DOE'S MOTHER IN LAW LOUNGE
☎ 504-947-1078; 1500 N Claiborne Ave

This is like a juke joint dedicated to the memory of soul singer Ernie K-Doe. His widow, Antoinette, runs it. There are live shows occasionally, and otherwise the jukebox is great, with plenty of K-Doe on it.

BLUE NILE
☎ 504-948-2583; 534 Frenchmen St

Nightly shows in this Marigny spot often begin early, around 5pm, and usually feature blues, jazz and R&B artists.

SHOPPING

LOUISIANA MUSIC FACTORY
☎ 504-586-1094; 210 Decatur St

Shoppers reemerge from this place with CDs by the sackful. The specialty here is Louisiana music, but the blues section is also very good.

JIM RUSSELL'S RARE RECORDS
☎ 504-522-2602; 1837 Magazine St

Serious collectors are drawn to this dense emporium, with its bottomless collection of vintage 45rpm discs, plus new and used CDs.

INDEX